Four Corners

Looking Back on 100 Years

Stories told in essays, poetry and verse

Maria Sangiolo

Salamander Publishing

Pomfret, Connecticut

ISBN: 979-8-9912445-0-3 (Hardcover)

Library of Congress Registration Number: Pending

Edited by Jamie Shaw
Front cover and family trees designed by Nancy McMerriman
Original watercolors by Talia R. Jessurun
Book & cover layout and design by Barry Jessurun

Printed by Ingram Spark in the United States of America.

~First printing edition 2024~

Salamander Publishing
P O Box 285
Pomfret, CT 06258

www.mariasangiolo.com

TABLE OF CONTENTS

DE LORENZO FAMILY TREE

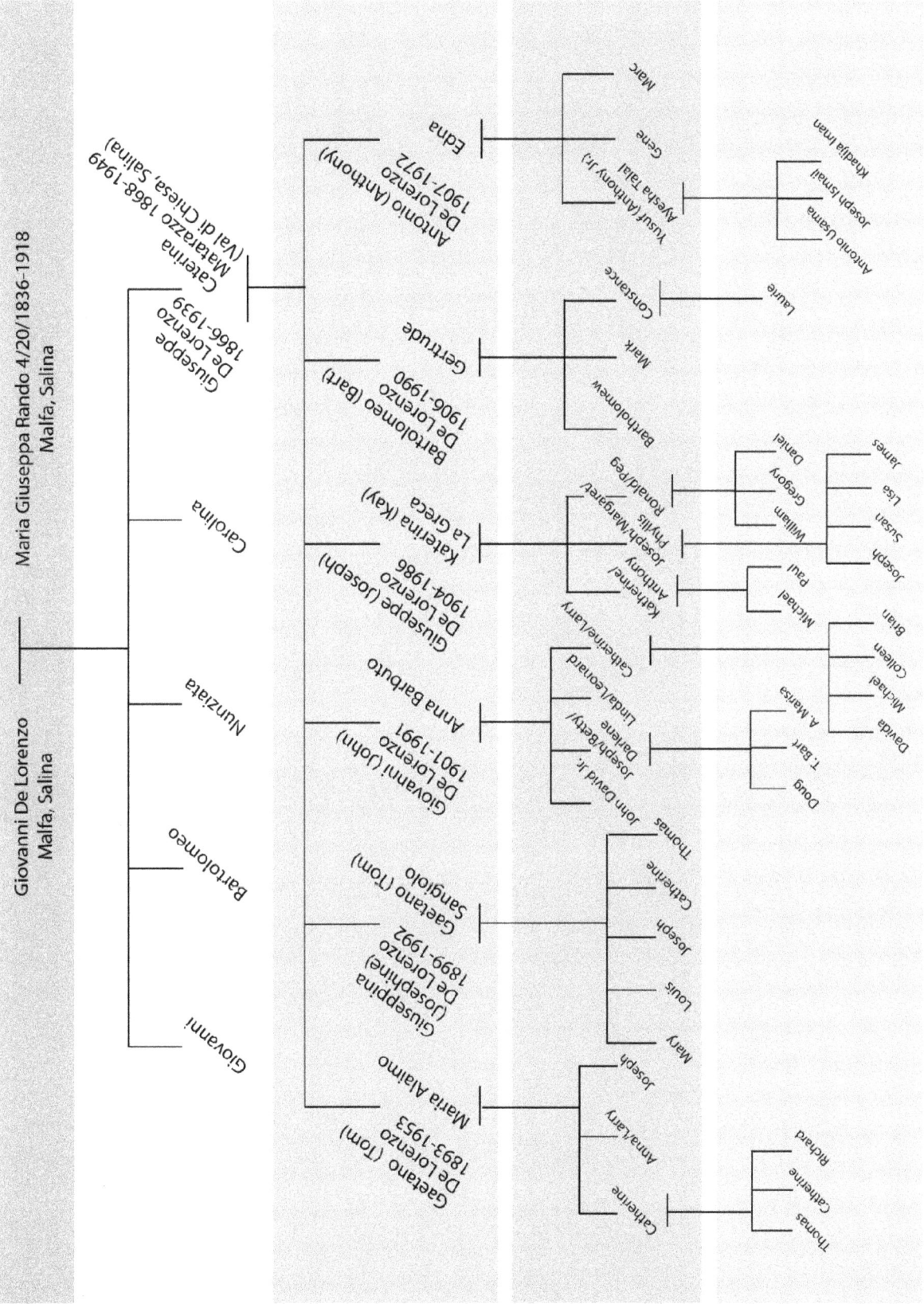

Giovanni De Lorenzo
Malfa, Salina

Maria Giuseppa Rando 4/20/1836-1918
Malfa, Salina

Giuseppe De Lorenzo 1866-1939
Caterina Matarazzo 1868-1949
(Val di Chiesa, Salina)

Carolina

Nunziata

Bartolomeo

Giovanni

Antonio (Anthony) De Lorenzo 1907-1972
Edna

Bartolomeo (Bart) De Lorenzo 1906-1990
Gertrude

Giuseppe (Joseph) De Lorenzo 1904-1986
Katerina (Kay) La Greca

Giovanni (John) De Lorenzo 1901-1991
Anna Barbuto

Gaetano (Tom) De Lorenzo 1899-1992
Giuseppina (Josephine) De Lorenzo

Gaetano (Tom) De Lorenzo 1893-1953
Maria Alaimo

Yusuf (Anthony Jr.)
Ayesha Talal
Gene
Marc

Antonio Usama
Joseph Ismail
Khadija Iman

Constance
Laure

Mark
Bartholomew

Kathrine/
Anthony
Joseph/Margaret
Phyllis
Ronald/Peg
William
Gregory
Daniel

Michael
Paul

Joseph
Susan
Lisa
James

Catherine/Larry
Linda/Leonard
Joseph/Betty/
Darlene
John David Jr.
Thomas

Doug
T. Bart
A. Marisa
Davida
Michael
Colleen
Brian

Thomas
Catherine
Joseph
Louis
Mary

Catherine
Anna/Larry
Joseph

Thomas
Catherine
Richard

iii

SANGIOLO FAMILY TREE

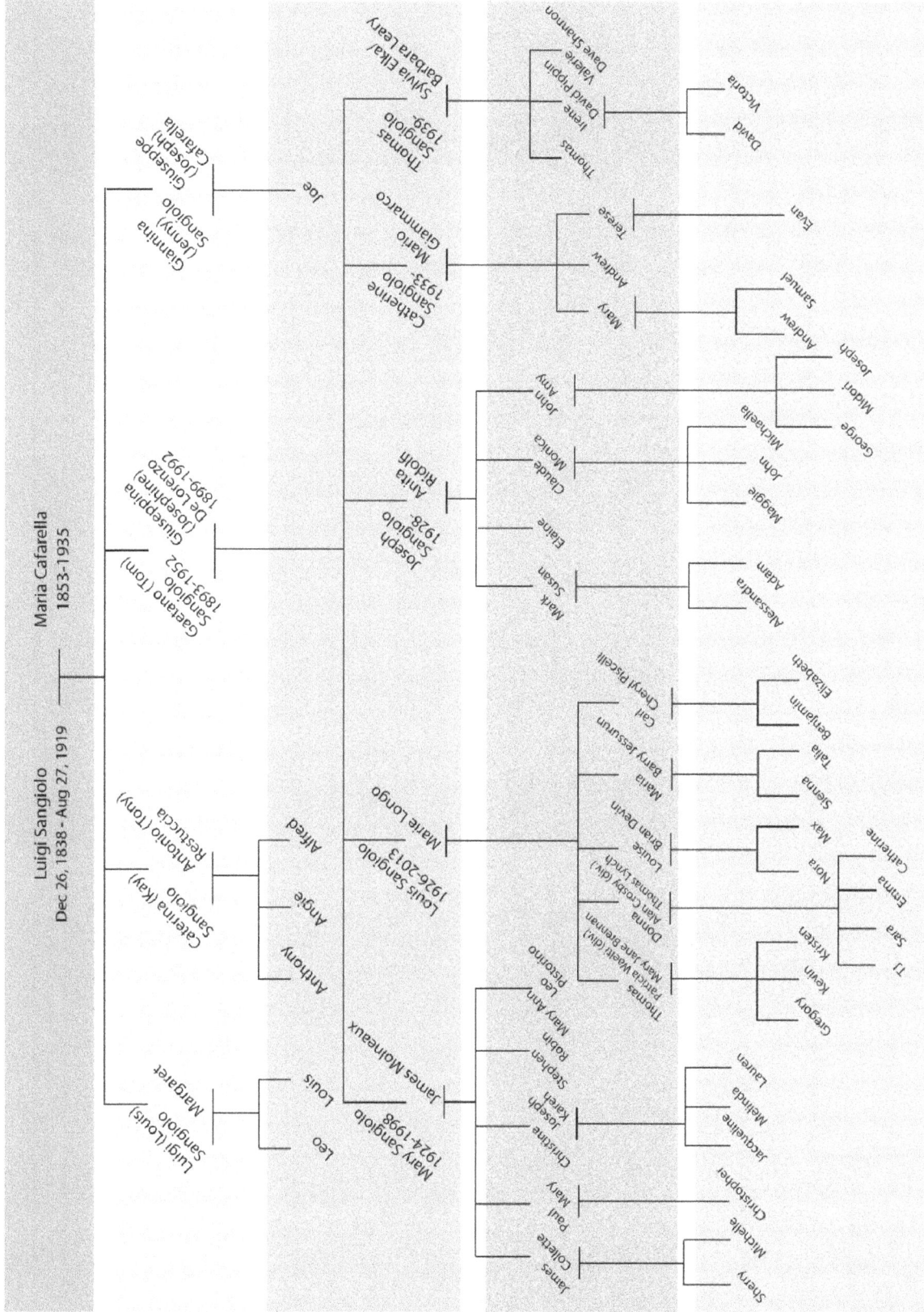

Luigi Sangiolo
Dec 26, 1838 - Aug 27, 1919

Maria Cafarella
1853-1935

Giuseppe (Joseph) Cafarella

Giannina (Jenny) Sangiolo

Joe
- Thomas Sangiolo 1939 / Sylvia Elka/ Barbara Leary
  - Irene Pippin / David Pippin
  - Thomas
  - Valerie / Dave Shannon
    - David
    - Victoria
- Mario Giammarco 1933- / Catherine Sangiolo 1933-
  - Mary
    - Midori
    - Joseph
    - Andrew
    - Samuel
  - Andrew
  - Terese
    - Evan

Giuseppina (Josephine) De Lorenzo 1899-1992

Gaetano (Tom) Sangiolo 1893-1952

- Anita Ridolfi 1928- / Joseph Sangiolo
  - Mark / Susan
    - Alessandra
    - Adam
  - Elaine
  - Claude / Monica
    - Maggie
    - John
    - Michaella
    - George
  - John / Amy

Caterina (Kay) Sangiolo

Antonio (Tony) Restuccia

- Alfred
- Angie
- Anthony

Louis Sangiolo 1926-2013 / Marie Longo
- Cheryl Piscelli / Carl
  - Benjamin
  - Elizabeth
- Maria / Barry Jessunun
  - Talia
  - Sienna
- Louise / Brian Devin
  - Max
  - Nora
- Donna Crosby (div) / Alan Crosby (div) / Thomas Lynch
  - Gregory
  - Kevin
  - Kristen
  - TJ
  - Sara
  - Emma
  - Catherine
- Thomas Wehrli (div) / Patricia Brennan / Mary Jane Brennan

Margaret

Luigi (Louis) Sangiolo
- Louis
- Leo

Mary Sangiolo 1924-1998 / James Moineaux
- Leo Pistorino / Mary Ann
- Robin
- Stephen / Karen
- Joseph / Christine
  - Jacqueline
  - Melinda
  - Lauren
- Paul / Mary
  - Christopher
- James / Colette
  - Michelle
  - Sherry

Preface

After my father died of Non-Hodgkin's Lymphoma in 2013, I attempted to write his life story to somehow keep him alive. But the grief lingered on, and the story was too heavy, so I abandoned the writing.

Three years flew by, but I was still not able to let him go. I started writing again, this time telling his parents' story. Their immigrant story was known and passed down to me from my aunt Catherine and my paternal grandmother, Josephine (Giuseppina) De Lorenzo Sangiolo, the matriarch of our large Italian American family. In her last years, I visited her on Sundays with my father at the Plymouth Manor Nursing Home, and it was there that I first learned her mother's family name *Matarazzo*. She wrote it out for me on a piece of yellow-lined legal paper. I have been collecting and recording oral stories about our extended family ever since. Her youngest daughter Catherine's storytelling informed much of this book. The more stories I collected the more it became apparent that I wanted to find a way to pass them on. Except for Native Americans and enslaved people, most Americans have an immigrant story, a shared history.

These stories span over one hundred years and are mostly true. There is no plot, no protagonist, just a recorded and remembered history. They tell my paternal grandmother's life story from the time she left Italy to when she became a widow at age fifty-three. I enlisted poetic license when I did not know certain details. This book provides a window into an immigrant experience around the turn of the 20th century; it will give a glimpse of a more family-centered society in both Italy and America. Family is forever.

For my father, Louis Anthony Sangiolo and my children.

Talia Jessurun and Papa Louis Sangiolo

Home, October 2023

"Grief was the celebration of love; those who could feel real grief were lucky to have loved."

Chimamanda Ngozi Adichie

I want to go home

to my childhood home

where I belong,

260 Atkinson Avenue in Stoughton, Massachusetts.

I want to visit my father

        and mother,   join them,

sit together on the island   Dad built,

see the kitchen Mom   designed.

We will talk about news of the family,

eat pasta, drink beer

        and wine.

When the visit is over,

they will stand at the front door,

    waving goodbye,

as I turn down the driveway one last time.

Please, take me home,

home to my extended family

where I belong, where we belong   to one another.

I miss my cousins, aunts, uncles,

and Noni.

There are so many grandnieces and grandnephews now.

Let's gather them all together,

make time for family again,

have a big reunion under the old white pine trees

like we did when we were young

in Duxbury.

I want to go home.

To our ancestral home Malfa

on the island of Salina, Sicily,

     where I belong.

        where we belong.

where the people look like me, look like us.

Know how to say our names -

Matarazzo, De Lorenzo, Sangiolo.

I will not be the only Sangiolo on Salina.

Sangiolo is an old island name.

Take me back home.

The Storyteller

While family stories were told to me by my father and his brothers, my father's sister Catherine was the family storyteller. With humor and the artistry of an actor, she held me captive as she retold memories of my paternal grandmother and the tales and escapades of her siblings in the store, Sangiolo and Sons in Dorchester, Massachusetts. Closing her eyes, hand in the air, and after a pause with dramatic effect as she recalled stories from the past she would say, "Now let me think."

On my first trip to Malfa, Salina, our ancestral home off the coast of Messina, Sicily, I traveled with my father's siblings and cousins. At one point, I thought to myself, *who are these people? My father could not be from the same family!* His siblings were so funny and entertaining in contrast to my father's quiet, more serious personality. Dad had a beautiful smile that lit up the room, but telling jokes or funny stories was not his forte. Over meals and long walks through that small island town, Aunt Catherine's stories almost told themselves, and raucous laughter filled the spaces between each tale. I was blessed with being her roommate and had a voice recorder on my phone that I pulled out as she put on her make-up every morning.

One morning Catherine recalled Noni returning to Salina for the first time in 1962. Miguele Alaimo, the cousin who purchased the DeLorenzo home for one dollar that year, was not home when she first arrived. Noni noted his dirty socks on the line with holes and said, "You'd think they would have been discarded." The chickens in the yard had hardly any feathers, plucked for harvest before their time. Then Catherine turned and said, "My mother used to say, 'who needs to shave your legs, the hair is only going to fall out. Look at me, I am like an old plucked hen!'"

It was at that moment that I knew I must put these stories down on paper. Noni lived to be almost ninety-four, and her idiomatic phrases were all her own. Noni had one-liners that would stop you in your tracks while laughing. She used to say, "Every time I take a bath I shrink-a like-a wool."

On the trip, the stories were full of humor but also wisdom and lessons. "'Life is not for sissies," Catherine once said. "Life is quite an adventure." Catherine celebrated her ninetieth birthday in March of 2023. She now lives in an assisted care facility in Falmouth, Massachusetts. I am so glad I reached for that voice recorder.

These stories, collected over my lifetime, grew into this body of work. They shape who I am, a descendant of the twentieth century Italian American immigrant story. Catherine and my father both said that one day they were going to write a book. My hope is that their voices live on in these pages.

Chapter One: The Sea and the Mountain

Malfa, Salina - The Aeolian Islands, Sicily, Spring 1912

"Caterina Matarazzo was born into a family that raised grapes for winemaking. She learned in early childhood that one truly reaps what they sow."   Edna De Lorenzo

Malfa Morning

I imagine their day of departure.

Giuseppina awakened to a Salina sunrise,

heard a flutter of wings in the early morning breeze.

Pumice dust blew off the cliff as the first morning fishing boat arrived.

Birds flocked in tandem,

tiralee, tiralee trills, songbirds sung to one another to greet the morning.

White, foamy waves crashed beside the hull,

barely missing rocks that tumbled close to the cliff's edge

but did not fall.

She moaned, curling back into the dream.

Sun beams pierced the pillow, eyes crusty with memory.

It was time to wake,

time to leave.

Dawn on the sparkling sea,

orange-gold ball rising

on the horizon of Punta Scario Beach.

In the cold, May morning

she warmed her hands by crackling coals inside her Mama Caterina's bread oven.

Its clay, oval shape smiled back at her on the veranda.

She could almost hear malvasia grapes growing, tender, purple caper buds blooming.

She was blooming.

turning twelve moons in August.

Could her brothers see the moons budding beneath her cotton dress?

She swept the earthen floor of the dusty kitchen, Caterina's only daughter.

Beloved verdant island spring.

Sipped fresh spring water from the cistern on the veranda.

Snapped a ripe fig and held the sun-ripened sweetness on her tongue.

Chewing that small fruit from her garden for the last time,

Mama Caterina called,

"Giuseppina! Where are your brothers? Wake them up, it is time to leave!"

Giuseppina packed up their belongings, and her four little brothers:

Giovanni age 11, Giuseppe age 7, Bartolomeo age 6, and Antonio age 4.

Their oldest brother Gaetano left for America when he was eighteen,

to work alongside Papa at the Plymouth Cordage Company.

Fitfully boarding the brig *Annina D'Albora*, a two-masted, square-rigged ship, they sailed to the mainland.

Mama Caterina called out, "Giuseppina hold Antonio's hand!

Giovanni, Giuseppe, Bartolomeo, behave!"

The Tyrrhenian Sea was kind that day.

Gentle, rolling waves sailed the brig across the water.

Departing the docks of Santa Marina Bay,

She left her home behind, her Nona, and friends.

"Ciao Nonna, Ciao me cugina Carolina, Ciao Salina."

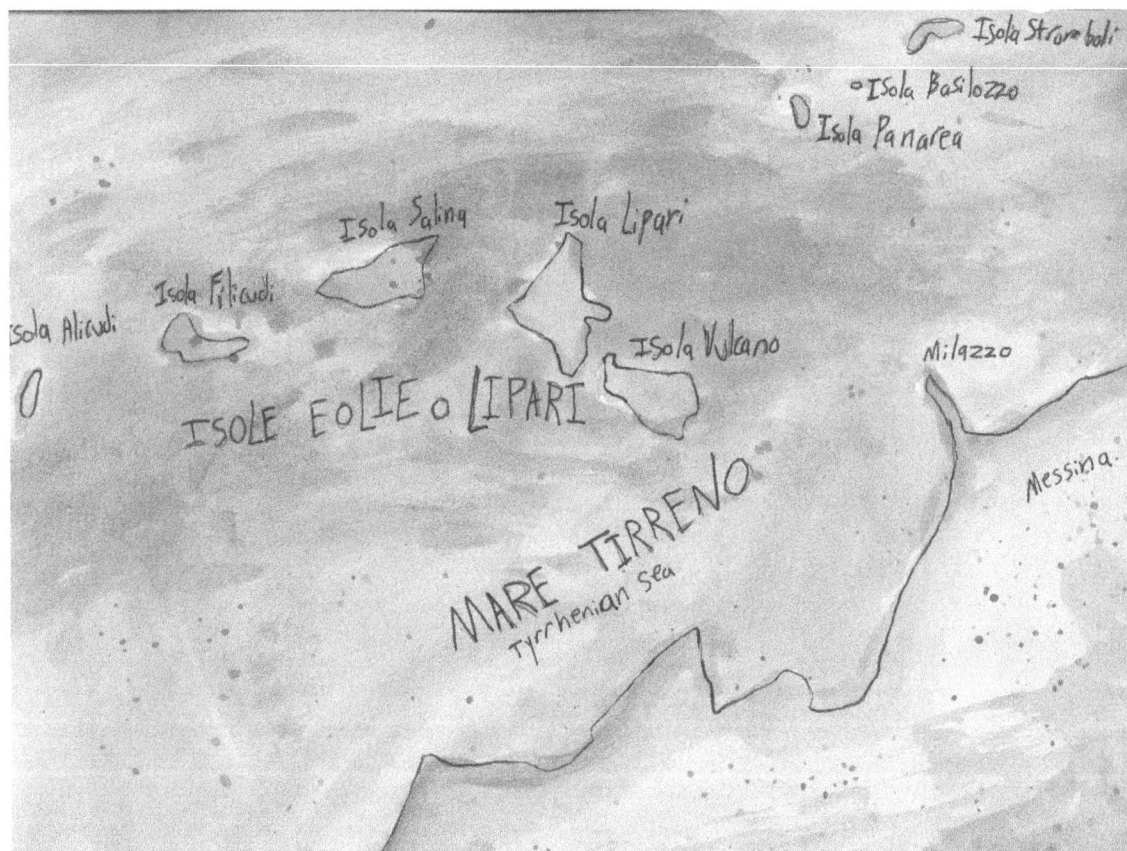

The Aeolian Islands, off the coast of Messina, Sicily, Naples to the northeast.

The ocean mist formed salty tears, trickling down to her mouth.

She watched the familiar volcanic mountains become smaller and smaller.

Hands high in the air, she heard the church bells ringing from the Immacolata,

prayed to the blessed virgin like an expectant bride.

Please God, watch over us on this long journey.

She was not sad to leave. There was nothing for them here.

The Phylloxera aphid destroyed the island's Malvasia grapevines and their livelihood.

4

Hitched a ride from the U.S.A. to all of Europe and Sicily on canes used to prop the grapes.

Sailed on ships miles across the sea to Salina in 1888, attacking the roots of the vines.

Papa left in 1900.

Salina's three mountains stared back, questioning her heart.

Majestic and ever green, like the heavenly Father, Son, and Holy Spirit.

In the distance Stromboli's smoke curled into the sky.

Giovanni said,

"Sis, look at the smoke rising into the clouds!

That old volcano is gonna blow! Vulcano, too!"

Panarea, little Filicudi, Alicudi, Grand Lipari was last.

No more fishing boat rides with Mama Caterina

to the markets on la Isola Grande di Lipari.

A new life was waiting, far across the sea.

Mama Caterina said,

 "Bambini, we are going on un-Aventura Grande to America."

Grudgingly, she smiled.

She never planned to leave her farm, her island home.

She wanted to live and work on these verdant hills forever.

There was a distant dream in her eyes.

And hope.

And strength.

She continued,

"Papa will be waiting and big brother Gaetano.

We will see a tall lady in New York harbor,

she will greet us, welcome us, make us feel safe."

Messina, Sicily – Port of Departure

Antonio, Bartolomeo, Giuseppe and Gianni

The boys were as restless as four caught fish.

"I'm hungry," said Giovanni.

"How long is this boat ride?" asked Giuseppe.

"Mama, when will be there?" asked Bartolomeo.

"I want to go home," said little Antonio.

They arrived in Messina just in time to hastily board the steamship.

Thanks to her baby brothers, they were always late.

Crowds of hungry migrants, leaving Sicily, waited on the dock.

There was no work, no Malvasia grapes to trade, no reason to stay.

Children cried to their parents, lifting them into tired arms, carrying just one worn leather satchel,

holding tickets to sleep at the bottom of the boat,

crammed together in steerage like sardines.

The De Lorenzos owned two pyramidal leather trunks.

Giovanni and Giuseppe

proudly carried them up to the state rooms,

beds to sleep in for the long journey.

It took nine days to sail to America.

No steerage, Mama Caterina saved the money her husband sent,

and his mother, Nonna Rando, helped buy their tickets.

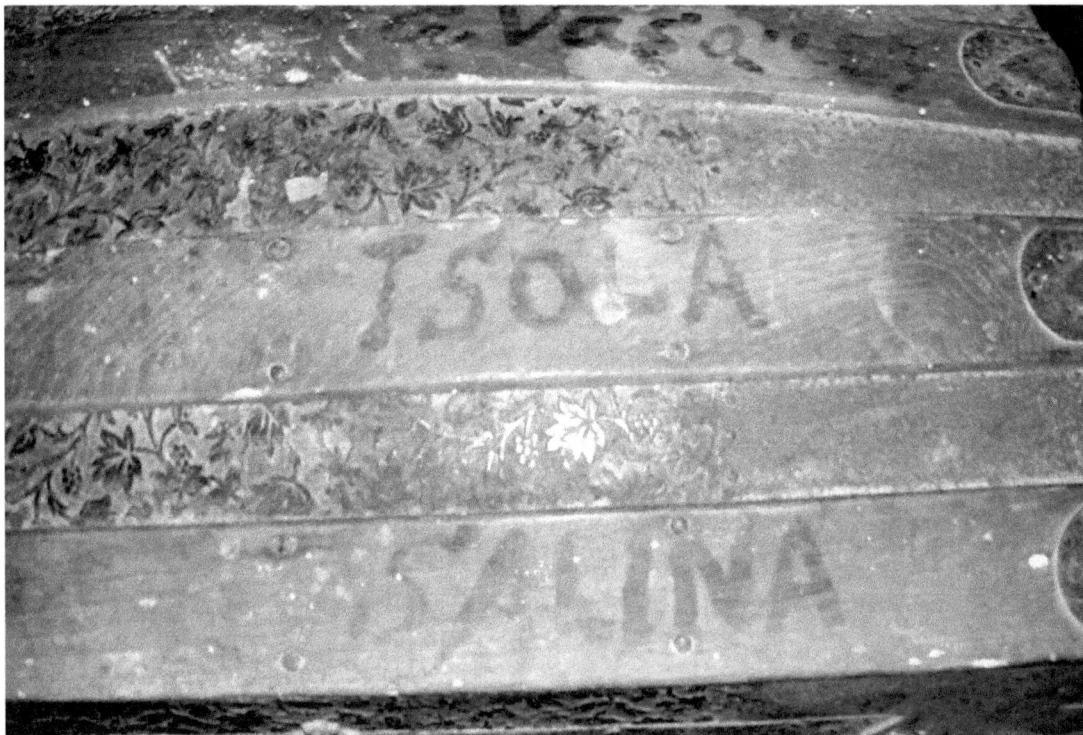

Papa Giuseppe De Lorenzo (my great-grandfather)

Before he left for America, he escorted his sisters Carolina and Nunziata to Australia.

Giuseppe De Lorenzo sailed on the ship *Bolivia* and paid $30 for his first passage to America in 1900.

His occupation: sailor.

Nonna Rando his mother,

an educated midwife from a prominent island family.

His father, Giovanni De Lorenzo, a merchant mariner.

He worked as a sailor on his father's ship in the Mercante di Mare.

Giuseppina was only a toddler when her papa left, hundreds of men were leaving, to find work.

Her mama said he was handsome, kind, and strong,

a fun-loving, easy-going, quiet gentleman.

"Yes, dear," he would reply to Mama Caterina.

Giuseppina, now twelve,

taught her baby brothers about Papa, for he was a stranger to them all.

"Papa earns six dollars a week at Plymouth Cordage working six days," she told the boys.

"What is Plymouth Cordage?" asked Bartolomeo.

"A rope factory," replied Gianni.

Giovanni, now age ten said, "He wires three dollars home a month,

keeps three dollars for himself and Gaetano.

9

Papa brings cash to the telegraph office.

Sends Mama Caterina a message,

and wires the funds to our bank on Salina."

Giovanni had a good business sense for a young boy.

It had been twelve years since Papa left for the United States.

Soon they will see him for more than a monthly visit every few years.

He will be their papa, every day.

Mama Caterina will stop being so grumpy with Papa home.

Giuseppina can be a child again,

and play all day with her China doll.

Recently, they learned Papa had had an accident,

cut his eye with a banana knife in the grocery.

Now he has one glass eye, he is partially blind.

Mama Caterina never wanted to leave Salina. NEVER.

At age 45, through mutual decree of her mother, her sister the nun, and the parish priest,

she made plans to leave her beloved island and join her husband.

"You belong with your husband,

go, go, and take care of him."

They told Caterina, "Your place is by your husband's side, especially now.

Three Remarkable Women

"The women on Salina are more dominant than you see anywhere, and it is tradition to keep their maiden names." William Cafarella Mitchell

Our female ancestors were remarkable women in their time. The mother, wife, and daughter of my great-grandfather Giuseppe De Lorenzo ran businesses, managed households, and raised children concurrently in the late 19th and early 20th century. Their lives knew hardship but also adventure, enduring love, and, for one, a formal education.

Maria Giuseppa Rando, his mother, earned a Diploma in Midwifery at an institution in Naples in the early 1800s. Her training was equivalent to a medical doctor; thus, she held a powerful position in the community of Malfa, equal to that of the mayor, postmaster, and priest. She traveled by fishing boat to attend births and treat other disorders. Later, her daughter Annunziata accompanied her, also a trained midwife. While we know Rando's family came from the island of Filicudi, we do not know how she met her husband, Giovanni De Lorenzo. However, our Noni (Giuseppina) spoke of how much she adored her paternal grandmother. Over twelve years, Rando paid for her son's travels to and from America on four separate occasions so he could visit his young family.

Caterina Matarazzo, his wife, was born into a family of winemakers in Val di Chiesa (Valley of the Church), Salina, and worked in the vineyard. Salina has always been known as the most verdant island of the Aeolian archipelago and still is today. Caterina learned how to grow Malvasia grapes, dry them in the sun and press them for wine and was well known for her fresh produce at the local market in Malfa. When her husband Giuseppe left for America in 1900, she ran the farm in Italy alone and, later, in Duxbury, Massachusetts. She worked in the fields from dawn until dusk and "never expected any task to be easy: indeed, it was unworthy of her attention if it was." She once told her granddaughter, Catherine Sangiolo, that she was "lazy and would never amount to anything because all she did was look in the mirror." Catherine feared her grandmother and did not like to be around her and her mean disposition. My father Louis once said that his grandmother was a tough bitch, and my second cousin, Linda De Lorenzo, recalled the day they took Caterina out and away from her farm in her last years to live with Noni and her family in Dorchester. I'm certain she was happy to see her leave.

His only daughter Giuseppina (Josephine) aka Noni embodied the loving, kind wisdom of her grandmother Rando, the humor of her father, and the fortitude of her 'Goliath' of a mother. Giuseppina was not allowed to get her fingernails dirty on the farm. Her work was in the home tending to her baby brothers, learning to knit and crochet, and minding the kitchen. In her one hundred years, she witnessed the advent of the industrialization of the United States and the end of our agrarian society. Imagine being a young teenage immigrant daughter from a small island courted by a handsome young man in his Model T Ford each Sunday. It must have been a thrill to ride alongside him as a passenger in his automobile after walking mountainous dirt roads, even if she had to be escorted by her brother John. Television, radio, toaster, clothes washer, dryer, perambulator, bicycle, and tractor were some of the many everyday conveniences invented in her lifetime. Raising her own two daughters during the rage of the roaring twenties must have been a constant challenge to her traditional Italian values, where girls lived at home until they wed, and marriages were arranged and approved by their fathers.

Raising her two daughters was uncharted territory for someone trained and self-taught, exclusively in the art of herding growing boys. Modern girls and their dreams were a mystery. Noni used to ask me, "When are you going to get married and have a baby," when I was still in high school. Giuseppina, Noni, was married to her husband, and the store, where she raised her children while waiting on customers. My father, Louis, used to play on the floor behind the counter with old peach baskets, building structures to pass the time. Noni's attention must have been divided between household and store responsibilities, and her children were indeed found at the other end of a wooden spoon when she lost her patience. But she did what she had to do and enjoyed working alongside her husband, greeting and servicing the local customers of the Dorchester *Four Corners*.

Concepts such as suffrage, women's rights, and women's liberation never entered our female ancestors' realities. However, they were strong, independent, and intelligent by nature. Aeolian women were equal partners to their merchant mariner or winemaker husbands and worked at home mending sails, salting fish, making malvasia wine, growing produce, and raising children. Aeolian women also kept their maiden names.

These three women in our lineage inform who we are today.

Chapter Two: A New Life, A New World

Nonna Rando: The Midwife

My great-great grandmother, Maria Giuseppa Rando

Nonna held Giuseppina close when they said goodbye,

like she was never going to see her again.

Giuseppina did not want to let her go.

> "Will we ever see her again?" asked Giuseppina.

Mama Caterina only smiled, holding out her strong arms to comfort her daughter.

Or was Giuseppina comforting Caterina?

> "Nonna will not leave for America, she has work to do."

Giuseppina loved her Nonna's soft, wrinkled hands.

Hands she held when they walked to church.

Hands that delivered so many babies,

Hands whose fast fingers formed orecchiette pasta, little ears.

Hands that wrapped her long, grey hair into a bun at the nape of her neck.

She was one of the midwives for the seven islands.

She and Aunt Carolina studied in Naples, a big education for women in the 1860s.

Nonna Rando delivered babies with herbal wisdom,

> like a goddess doctor.

She delivered all six De Lorenzo children.

After Papa's visits, Mama Caterina's belly grew big and round.

Four more babies came over twelve years.

Giuseppina knew how babies were born, thanks to Nonna Rando.

The Phylloxera: Mariners, Farmers, and Grocers

The De Lorenzos and Sangiolos were forced to abandon their livelihoods.

When the Phylloxera aphid destroyed the Malvasia grapevines on Salina, "Their shipping business in the Mercanti di Mare was sunk," wrote Yusuf De Lorenzo.

Giovanni De Lorenzo and Luigi Sangiolo's maritime trading ceased when canes from Sicily, used to prop the Malvasia grapevines, carried the aphid to Salina in 1888. The pest had traveled all the way from the U.S.A. The nine thousand prosperous island inhabitants lost their livelihood. During the great migration that number dwindled down to the hundreds. The insect had previously destroyed the vineyards of Europe and all of Sicily. The islanders never thought it would travel twenty-five miles across the sea to Salina. But it succeeded. All trade and transport of goods slowly ceased on the privately-owned boats by Aeolian men, Mercanti di Mare – the Maritime Mariners.

The Mariners built, maintained, and sailed ships to trade the beloved Malvasia wine, capers, pumice, and sea salt harvested on the Aeolian islands to ports in southern Europe along the coasts of Sicily. Luigi Sangiolo carried barrels of malvasia wine on his shoulder down the winding mountain path from his vineyard to the 'magazines' on the shore for storage. When filled, he would make plans to set sail. Wives wove flax and mended sails, salted food for travel, and maintained accounting for the business while caring for children and performing household chores. The aphid caught them unaware, overtaking their livelihood, and left them starving. And so, our ancestors migrated to Australia and The United States of America.

A similar thing happened to the Duxbury farm(s) twice, once with the oncoming of grocery stores and again when huge producers like Purdue took over the poultry market, leveraged economies of scale to bring lower costs, pricing small producers out of the market. Also, the arrival of the First National Supermarket across the street from Sangiolo and Sons grocery forced my paternal grandfather into retirement.

Giovanni De Lorenzo had connections in the rope-making business and helped young Giuseppe by paying his passage to America to work for the Plymouth Cordage Company. Gaetano Sangiolo arrived in New York with his brother Luigi with nothing but the shirt on his back. Their big sister Cay (Caterina Sangiolo) was living in New York with her husband Anthony Restuccia and helped her brothers get acclimated. Arriving in America did offer the promise of a better life and potential work but there were no streets paved in gold like those promoted on shiny posters.

Gaetano Sangiolo used to free dive for octopus to feed his family on the island. He once said soon after he arrived in New York, that "if he had the money, he would have returned home to Salina." Living conditions in the big city when he arrived in 1909 were horrendous for immigrants. He was homeless and slept under his fruit stand until he saved enough to move to Boston.

But for our industrious ancestors, small business would provide a comfortable life for the family. The DeLorenzo children worked on the farm and the Sangiolo children in the store.

Luigi Sangiolo, my paternal great grandfather, ship's captain in the Mercanti di Mare.

'Magazines' for storage in Capo Faro on the Island of Salina.

Ellis Island, New York, Summer 1912

It took nine long days to get to America.

The tall lady was standing in the harbor, waiting,

just like Mama Caterina said.

A sign said, 'Give me your tired, your poor, your huddled masses yearning to breathe free…'

Their ship docked on Manhattan Island.

Giuseppina was so happy to finally get off the ship and out of the small cabin with her little brothers.

The De Lorenzos could not speak English.

Someone who spoke Italian translated,

told them to board a small ferry to a hospital on Ellis Island.

They arrived at lines forming in every direction, like cow stalls.

So many strange-looking people, waiting to see a doctor.

Finally, they were inspected like Mama's goats, poked and prodded,

to make sure they were not carrying a disease from Salina.

If passengers were sick, they sent you right back,

and they paid for the return ticket.

They stood in endless lines all day.

"Mama where is Papa, when will we go to Boston?" asked Giovanni.

"I'm hungry, my legs hurt, why are there so many people?" the boys complained.

So many questions. The boys wanted to play. Giuseppina just wanted to get to Boston.

After long, hot, dusty hours wandering like sheep,

they were permitted to enter the United States.

They were all healthy.

 "Whew!" said Mama Caterina. "Grazi a Dio!"

They rode the passenger ferry back to New York City.

America did not pave the streets in gold.

Rats the size of rabbits passed them on the sidewalk,

like the ones Papa hunted on Salina.

Mama Caterina scolded, "Giuseppina! hold Antonio's hand!"

Why, she could just spank her little brother, he was always getting away!

Trying to stay together, they made their way through crowds of immigrants,

men dressed in dark suits, women in fancy dresses wearing hats with colorful bird feathers,

in a shiny new place called Grand Central Station.

They boarded a train to Boston.

There were people selling fruit on carts in the station.

Giuseppina's tummy growled.

"What are all those pretty colors?" asked Giovanni.

They reminded the children of the market where Mama Caterina sold vegetables in Malfa.

Mama Caterina could not read or write,

but she could figure numbers in her head when she added up a sale,

like a computer.

They did not take the capers, or the Malvasia grapevines with them.

There were no living grapevines left on the island and no plants allowed on the ship.

Mama Caterina worked hard for so many years, saving the money Papa sent,

Harvesting food to provide for them while Papa worked far away in America.

Mama Caterina said, "Children, we will have a farm again, one day."

Papa Giuseppe

My great-grandfather the rope maker

(Ropewalks were a familiar feature of almost every seaboard town. By 1810, Plymouth Cordage was one of 173 ropewalks in the United States.)

Papa left for America in 1900 when Gaetano was six and Giuseppina just a baby.

The Phylloxera had come to Italy.

There was no need for the merchant mariners, Mercante di Mare, anymore.

Traders' families were starving.

Giuseppe's father, Giovanni DeLorenzo knew someone in the states,

got Papa a job as a laborer at the Plymouth Cordage Company in Plymouth, Massachusetts.

On July 1st, 1900, Papa Giuseppe, a sailor, arrived on Ellis Island.

His mother, Nonna Rando, paid $30 for his passage

aboard the ship *Bolivia* with his cousin Angelo Rando, also a sailor.

Plymouth Cordage specialized in ropemaking for ship rigging and Plymouth binder twine.

Papa received $1.00 a day.

He worked from sunup to sundown, six days a week.

The company founder, Bourne Spooner, called it free labor.

A direct descendant of the Pilgrims who colonized America,

Spooner did not believe in slavery.

He recruited laborers from all over Europe to work at the Cordage.

Papa was free, free to labor and worked twelve hours a day, six dollars a week.

The Ropewalk Dance

Papa wrapped the spun fibers of twine around his waist,

walking 110 feet, backward down the ropewalk,

twisting the fibers, like making yarn with three strands:

Papa did a ropemaking dance in a straight line.

      Fibers twisted right-handed into yarn,

           Yarn twisted left-handed in the strands,

      Strands twisted right-handed into rope.

           Twisted twine stored on pegs on the wall.

Papa said the twisting of fibers into rope was one of the oldest arts:

Ancient Egyptian, Chinese, Native American, Polynesian, Roman, Greek,

and Mr. Spooner's ancestors.

The Anglo-Saxons spun rope for centuries.

The Cordage

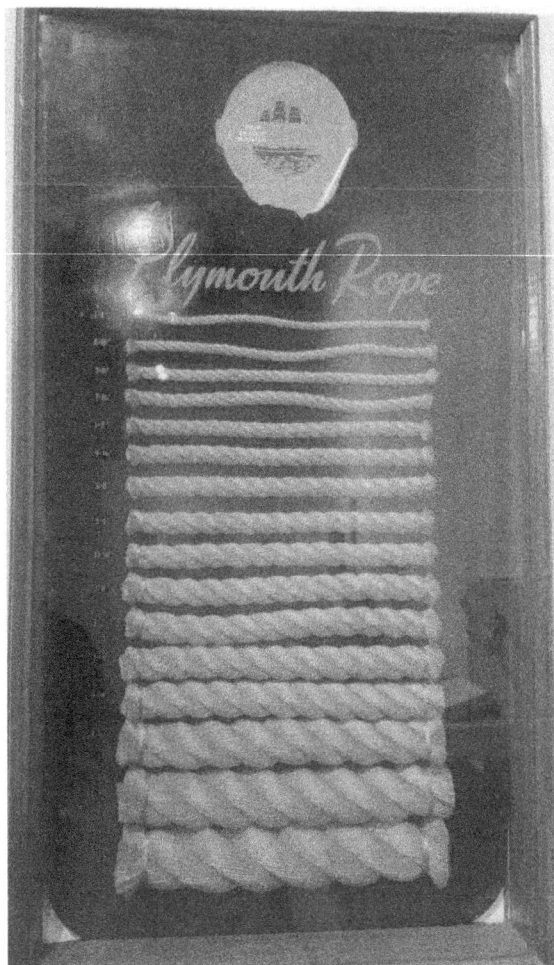

Plymouth Cordage was the largest manufacturer of rope and binder twine in the world.

The company provided tenement housing for employees,

but Papa Giuseppe lived in North Plymouth, the Italian part of town.

Like an indentured servant, he shopped in the company store where he bought:

butter for 19 cents a pound

flour for $6.25 a barrel

molasses for 48 cents a gallon

And New England rum for 48 cents a gallon.

He cut wood for fuel, caught cod and halibut for salting.

Salted fish and potatoes lasted him all winter.

Papa sent for his eldest son Gaetano to be an apprentice at the Cordage when he turned eighteen.

He was already married to Maria Grazia Alaimo,

whose family lived next door to the De Lorenzos on Salina.

Working at the Cordage, his son Gaetano received $35 dollars a year.

At 21, he got a factory job.

The immigrant workers at the factory were Italians, German, Portuguese,

English, Irish and Welsh,

French-Canadians and Americans.

Bartolomeo Vanzetti worked at the Cordage in 1913.

Soon the after the young De Lorenzo family arrived in the states,

Mama Caterina told Papa,

"No more Plymouth Cordage.

 I do not like these people.

Open a grocery store with Gaetano."

De Lorenzo Market

Atlantic (Quincy) MA

Papa Giuseppe De Lorenzo

Papa followed Mama Caterina's orders.

As always, he replied, "Yes, dear."

He and Gaetano opened a store,

Selling fruit and vegetables, pasta, and grocery items

In the new De Lorenzo Grocery.

There were small Italian-owned groceries on every corner in the Boston area.

The De Lorenzo's lived near Boston in Quincy,

a seaside town with many Italian immigrants.

So close to the ocean, they could smell the fish jumping in the water.

There was an accident in the store.

Papa Giuseppe poked his eye with a banana knife while working.

The hospital gave him a new glass eye; now he was partly blind.

This accident forced Mama Caterina to come to America to take care of Papa and Gaetano.

Mama Caterina never intended to leave Salina.

Nickelodeon

DeLorenzo Groceries, Atlantic, Quincy, MA

They lived upstairs from the store; Papa worked at the grocery with Gaetano.

Little shops sat on every corner.

Paesani, Italian immigrants, sold fruits and vegetables.

De Lorenzo's backyard was too small for even a garden patch.

     Mama Caterina was not happy.

Giuseppina was in the sixth grade when they arrived in Boston.

They went to a big, crowded school.

It was hard to make friends for they could not speak English very well.

One afternoon, five-year old Antonio stole a dime from Mama's purse,

skipped school and went to see a movie at Nickelodeon.

Antonio was always having adventures.

     Mama Caterina was furious.

She said, "Basta! Enough! This city is no place to raise children!"

She found an ad in the local paper for a fully furnished farmhouse for sale with fifteen acres.

A home in the country by the ocean, like their island home in Salina.

Her husband knew the area having worked in Plymouth.

They sent their oldest son Gaetano with a check for $2,000,

a lot of money in 1912.

Gaetano traveled by train on the Old Colony Line to Plymouth, then Duxbury,

on the south shore of Boston.

If he liked what he saw, he must pay the farmer in full that day.

And indeed, he liked what he encountered.

A quiet, rural town by the ocean, with fewer than 4,000 residents.

Mama Caterina and Giuseppe De Lorenzo signed the deed,

For a farmhouse and fifteen acres of land in West Duxbury.

Women could not own land in the United States until 1970.

The paper stated that it was part of her dowry in marriage.

Caterina was an equal landowner to her husband.

The Family Farm

When I was a child the De Lorenzo farm belonged to Uncle John, but it seemed to belong to everyone, even me, a Sangiolo, for we often gathered there as an extended family for parties and picnics.

Originally purchased in 1913 by my great-grandparents, Caterina Matarazzo and Giuseppe De Lorenzo, Sunny View Farm began as a fifteen-acre parcel in West Duxbury. At that time, only one other Italian family lived in Duxbury, the Navas. My great-grandparents moved their children from Quincy to the rural seaside town to escape the dangers of the Boston area. It was "no place to raise a child," said Mama Caterina.

Even after they subdivided parcels in 1939 between the boys, (first Giovanni and Giuseppe and later Antonio), three brothers competed for poultry customers, socialized, and were civil siblings. The De Lorenzo farms on Route 53 were three of the seven poultry farms known as Turkey Row, which supplied the Boston area chickens, then turkeys, for years until a man named Purdue changed all that. The brothers tried to convince younger brother Bart to return to Duxbury. An MIT graduate, he was an engineer and had a career and life in New York and later Ohio. The oldest brother Gaetano owned a grocery store in Medford. Giuseppina, the only daughter, did not receive land until years later.

Giuseppina, married to Gaetano Sangiolo in 1923, visited Duxbury every weekend with her husband and children when Gaetano took Sundays off. Like a summer housekeeper, she was always making beds and cleaning sheets, but she loved it. On Sundays, my father and his siblings begged their father to take them to the beach and their "Pa" never said no. Family picnics at Long Pond in Plymouth in the late 1920s, '30s and '40s were the summer's mainstay for my grandparents and their kids. Photos of women at the beach donning feathered hats and bathing suits to their knees was proof that life was rich with time for family. Sunday visits to Duxbury continued the tradition throughout my childhood when Dad took the day off to visit his uncles, take us to Duxbury Beach, and sometimes go fishing.

Our extended families gathered at the farm from the 1950s until the 1990s, for picnics in the trees, at Christmas or a family reunion in summer. When Uncle John passed away in his favorite chair, his daughter Linda continued the tradition. We even gathered twice at the Tar Kiln School down the road where the young De Lorenzo children attended a two-room schoolhouse. The family farm became everyone's farm and belonged to us all. But it was not always so sunny. Caterina was less than kind, brutally controlling, and not an easy person with whom to live, especially when she was mother, wife, grandmother, mother-in-law, and your boss. Farming was hard living.

Chapter Three: The Only Road to the Cape - Farm Tourism

Summer Street, Route 53, was the only road to Cape Cod from Boston, MA until 1963. The Old Colony Line ran six trains a day to the South Shore from 1871-1939. St. Joseph's Catholic Church in Kingston was the closest Roman Catholic parish, their church. Mama Caterina rode horseback to the grain and feed store in Kingston to shop. The bank, telegram, and grocer were also close by in Kingston.

Most Italians lived and worked in Plymouth for the Cordage. Did the settlers in South Duxbury not welcome the De Lorenzos? Louis Nardi from Boston owned The Briars in the Old Cobb's Tavern, a notorious speakeasy, a place for drinking and gambling. Nardi was one of a few Italians in Duxbury at that time.

Mama Caterina did not escape the dangers of the city. Perhaps, young men patronized the place for rum after school, while studying at Partridge Academy during Prohibition?

The De Lorenzos Move to Summer Street, West Duxbury, MA

Gianni, Papa, Mama, Giuseppina, Giuseppe Jr., Bartolomeo, Antonio, Gaetano

West Duxbury was and still is the agricultural part of town.

The wealthy folk live on the south bayside.

The De Lorenzo farmhouse was built in 1782.

The old, hired hand, Henry Martin, helped them unpack.

He showed Mama Caterina all the farm equipment: plow, harrow, tractor, and old truck.

They had an open-hearth fireplace in the family room.

Beyond the kitchen, there was a grape arbor, a peach tree, and an outhouse,

outside the back door with four holes.

They had a water pitcher and bed pan in each bedroom.

There was no heat upstairs; in winter, the boys woke with icicles on their chins.

Giuseppina's room was cozy and warm on the first floor, near the stove.

The boys treated their big sister with respect. She was like their second mother.

The De Lorenzo boys were gentlemen, like their Papa Giuseppe.

"Alla Nostra Tavola si Mangia Sempre Bene!

At our table, one always eats well!" said Mama Caterina.

They ate what they grew,

drank fresh milk from a cow they named Mayflower.

Dick the horse helped turn the soil,

pulling the plow in spring.

The boys learned to drive on the old tractor.

Mama Caterina rode the horse to buy grain in Kingston.

She baked bread and sold it to the men building Route 53 for ten cents a loaf,

to make extra money.

Cape travelers stopped at local farms

to buy fresh produce for their vacations.

Mama Caterina was a businesswoman.

Mama was a farmer.

Mama was uneducated.

Mama loved to feel the earth between her fingers.

Mama was smart.

Mama was frugal.

Fruits, Vegetables, Berries and Fresh Eggs

Papa Giuseppe built a roadside farm stand.

The sign said: *Sunny View Farm*

Fruits, vegetables, berries, and fresh eggs

In the chicken coops, the boys braved the old hens who pecked their fingers

as they collected eggs before school.

Papa milked the cows at four in the morning,

Mama weeded between the rows of vegetables in the scorching summer sun.

Always work, work, work to be done.

Mama Caterina kept the boys busy from sunup to sundown.

With the ocean nearby, they heard the killdeer and seagulls, smelled the salty air upon waking, just like Salina.

Mama rose early to bake the bread,

Papa Giuseppe entertained the customers with his humor.

Mama Caterina worked on the farm from dawn, in all weather.

"Boys, plant the tomatoes, no not that way, this way!

Giuseppina, wash the sheets and make the beds!

Company is coming on Sunday!" ordered Mama Caterina.

The farm was a weekend destination for family and friends,

and members of the Franciscan Society in the city, fellow Aeolians from the islands.

They had a grand piano in the living room,

But Mama would not let the children touch it.

The De Lorenzo children could not put anything on top of it.

The piano was there when they bought the house.

Mama Caterina polished it like silver.

Handstands

John and Joseph De Lorenzo, Gaetano Sangiolo, Anthony, and Bart De Lorenzo, 1932

Bartolomeo walked on his hands more than his feet.

People stopped to watch him on the beach, in the street,

to see the slender young man

with his feet

flying in the summer air.

He entertained Giuseppina,

and his brothers,

his mother and father,

his nieces and nephews.

Eccentric, gregarious,

fun-loving Pied Piper,

Effortless handstands,

debonair.

Five Boys and a Girl

Giuseppina was a petunia in an onion patch.

      Henry Martin said, "When you need to pee and poop,

      you go outside the back door to the outhouse."

The brothers liked to lock Giuseppina inside.

She enjoyed their humor.

Sometimes, they peed out the bedroom windows,

killing Mama Caterina's roses below.

Mama could never figure out why her flowers stopped blooming.

They would all laugh and have great fun together.

The boys called Giuseppina "Big Sis" and treated her like a queen.

The farmhouse had no plumbing, no electricity.

They cleaned wash basins and bed pans every morning.

The boys slept upstairs with no heat, but they were never sick.

They saw their breath upon waking; the cold kept their lungs clean.

Giuseppina slept downstairs outside the kitchen near the coal stove.

      Papa said, "You are my petunia in the onion patch."

The Plow and The Harrow

All winter they waited for the warmth to return to Duxbury. Bartolomeo read his books aloud; the boys would crochet as they listened to pass the time. When the last snow melted on the old barn, they began to plan. Mama ordered the seeds in February.

By April the red hawk, golden plover, hermit thrush and winter wrens arrived in spring; the berry patch needed weeding.

Mayflower the cow provided fertilizer composting in a pile they mucked from her stall. Brother Joseph, arms the size of tree trunks, rode behind Dick the horse as he dragged the plow, loosened the soil to prepare for the roots of crops. The horse pulled the harrow to break up and smooth the surface tillage, tilth to plant the seeds.

Horse-drawn planting required three of the boys: Giovanni to walk behind and lay the seed, Giuseppe to take control of the horse and plow, Bartolomeo to keep the weeds down in the furrow, a shallow trench of soil fell behind the plow. The old wooden plow was bolted together with metal bars.

Mama Caterina knew when it was time to plant, what to plant, where to plant. Papa just smiled and said, "Yes dear."

Education

My paternal great-grandmother said, "The boys have got to get an education." She understood that farming might not take care of their future. Education was a privilege, even for young men in the early twentieth century. Sunny View Farm paid for four of the De Lorenzo boys to go to college. Caterina was frugal and scrimped and saved. Her daughter never graduated from high school. Giuseppina learned to knit and crochet and take care of her baby brothers. Giuseppina (Josephine) loved babies. She did not want to go to school. It was 1913, and she was in the sixth grade when they left Quincy to move to Duxbury.

Once they entered school in Duxbury all the children used English names.

Tar Kiln School

The whitewashed, two-room schoolhouse stood on Route 53,

less than a half mile down the street from their new country home.

Two teachers instructed the class.

In Duxbury, the children adopted their American names.

They were American and learning to speak English.

Giuseppina, now Josephine, was the second oldest.

She and the four boys walked to school together.

Josephine completed eighth grade back home in Salina.

At the end of their first summer in Duxbury

They were enrolled in the Tar Kiln School

for children grades one through eight.

None of the De Lorenzo children spoke English, but the boys were young

and would learn fast.

They placed Josephine in the elementary classroom.

She was almost fourteen; she was so embarrassed.

Josephine Went to School, 1913

Josephine and her brothers walked to school together in a line:

she, then John, Joseph, Bartholomew, and Anthony.

In 1913, she was almost fourteen.

At home, they were all taught to trust in people,

to plant the seeds of faith in God and a love for life.

In school, Josephine could not find the right words to speak.

Italian her native tongue, English a mystery.

They placed her with the sixth-grade girls,

wearing bonnets, slippers, and hair tied in curls.

She was almost fourteen, not a girl.

Later, she stomped her feet on the kitchen floor.

"Please, Papa please, do not make me go to school anymore.

The girls whisper, they smile but are cruel,

They do not live by the Golden Rule."

Papa smiled, "Please Josephine, you must try."

She cried and cried, so ashamed.

The tallest in her class, the kids could not say her name.

Writing letters and numbers, reading *Dick and Jane*,

Made her feel small and helpless again.

She loved to learn, she loved school,

But did not like being treated like a young girl.

She begged her Papa, "Do not make me go back.

I am almost fourteen, I am taller at that!

I should be in the eighth grade, not in grade six."

But he told her, "Be patient, you must learn to speak English."

She tried her best every day,

but she would never fit in with the girls in sixth grade.

They stared at her body, they looked at her dress,

Her hair in a bun, her mood a mess.

Day after day, she begged and pleaded,

"Please, Papa, may I stay home on the farm?

The kitchen needs cleaning.

I am not a girl. I am almost fourteen!

Do not make me go back, please Papa please."

After many weeks, and an ocean of tears

Papa gave in and said, "Va benne, you can stay here,

But your brothers will teach you to speak English,

to write and to read."

Josephine smiled, for she loved to clean,

embroider, crochet, and cook.

She would learn to speak English and read a book.

She helped feed the boys while Mama Catarina ran the farm.

And every day, after their chores, her brothers helped her learn.

Josephine went to school, home school,

and she and her brothers lived by the Golden Rule.

They loved each other, their neighbors, friends,

and their new country.

They treated everyone they met with the utmost respect.

Unlike the girls in fine dresses and curls,

Josephine never graduated from Tar Kiln School.

The Spanish Flu of 1918, la Pesta

The Spanish Flu took the life of great-great grandmother Maria Giuseppa Rando, the midwife, in Italy.

The Spanish Flu came to Duxbury in late August of 1918, shutting down much of the town.

Josephine NEVER spoke of the atrocities.

They survived, if indeed the sickness reached her family.

Babies and children died in the arms of their mothers, overnight.

The odd virus acted quickly and horribly.

Sixteen people between the ages of 22 and 40 died.

At the time, Duxbury had a year-round population of 1,500.

The town swelled to four thousand residents in the summer months.

Schools, churches, and public gathering spots closed.

Angela Pray, a visiting nurse, helped residents cope with the pandemic.

They called her "an angel of mercy."

She came to the mothers who were tending the sick,

rolled up her sleeves and made a significant difference.

Milk, broth, and bedding committees worked to supply essentials,

for the young parents needing help caring for children.

In the city of Boston, where Josephine's future-betrothed Gaetano Sangiolo lived,

The city collected bodies in wagons, people left corpses on their front porches,

even on the sidewalks, buried so many dead in unmarked graves.

Reflection on Socialism: Sacco and Vanzetti: 1921- 1927

"My father liked Mussolini for what he did for Italy." Uncle Tom Sangiolo

Mussolini was the editor of a popular socialist magazine Avanti, primarily organizing with trade unions and writing for leftist publications. During WWI his politics shifted right with themes of racial superiority, Xenophobia, and imperialism. In April 1945, Italy's government arrested and hanged him along with his lover Clara Petacci, "Their bodies were strung up by their heels outside a service station in Milan." Wikepedia.org

Uncle Tony, the youngest of the De Lorenzo brothers, filed a document for naturalization to become a U.S. citizen in 1920 and had to sign a separate document stating that he was not an anarchist. His father and older brother Tom both worked at the Plymouth Cordage Company at the same time as Bartolomeo Vanzetti who lived nearby in North Plymouth. According to Yusuf De Lorenzo, Tony's eldest son, "None of our elders ever talked about the infamous case against these two Italian immigrants. Suffice to say, our grandmother Caterina found a haven for the family in Duxbury, far from the Irish cops in Boston and all the paranoia surrounding Italian immigrants. Her sons attended Partridge Academy next door to Duxbury Town Hall, where they learned to drink tea, eat biscuits, and observe all the niceties."

In Upton Sinclair's novel *Boston*, he states "Work life in the factories of America was full of danger and death for impoverished immigrant adults and young children. Between 1877 and 1914, the U.S. experienced the most violent rebellions of working people in the history of the modern state."

Sinclair wrote, "Plymouth Cordage was the greatest rope factory in the entire world and extended three quarters of a mile along Plymouth Bay, with a covered dock to which ships came to unload their cargoes of sisal to the nearby railroad tracks and switch yard for the cars to carry away rope and binder twine. When the screaming siren sounded in the morning, the great machines started to rumble. The workers would sit or stand, and make the same motions, repeatedly, day after day, for five hours straight. They had a one-hour break for lunch and then returned to their stations for another five hours until the siren sounded closing time at six pm. It took an intelligent person five minutes to learn all there was to the job and after that it was the same motion, over and over, at the mercy of an enormous machine" (Sinclair).

During the historic month-long strike of the Plymouth Cordage Company in 1916, Sinclair wrote, "a huddled mass of 2000 men and women speaking a dozen different languages, an unorganized mass, began to organize. On pay day Thursday, a dispute ignited the spark in the spinning room." Above it rose the word, "Strike!" "Sciopero!" yelled the Italians. "Folga!" echoed the Portuguese. "Greve!" shrieked the French-Canadians. "Streik!" bellowed the

Germans and "Strike! Strike! Strike!" roared Americans and English, Irish, and Welsh and all others who learned the word (Sinclair).

Sinclair continued, "Preceding the payday strike there appeared mysteriously at the cordage plant a force of two hundred and fifty 'private police' to guard the property. Where did they come from? Big husky fellows, bundled in overcoats and arctics and fur-topped gloves, with clubs in their hands and revolvers in holsters at their belts – in plain sight where nobody could miss their meaning" (Sinclair).

The various "gruppi" had agreed upon their demands, eight dollars a week for unskilled women and twelve for the men. The company explained at an organized meeting with their appointed committee that such an increase, twenty-five percent, would bankrupt it and then no one would have a job. Thus, the strike ensued.

Vanzetti had seen the trenches of World War I in Italy, saw men kill their own brothers and men die horrible deaths. He spoke out for the poor man. He denounced war and capitalism. He said to himself, "Don't be a traitor, speak the truth, make protest, make propaganda, get a meeting, call the men."

Sinclair wrote, "The socialists had a meeting-place in North Plymouth, Rispicci Hall, and this was thrown open and swarming with strikers. Impromptu meetings were held, and committees named, and speeches made. Sympathizers and propagandists from Boston came; Luigi Galleani and Bartolomeo Vanzetti, who formerly worked the factory and blamed his participation in the strike for being blacklisted in the region. Felice Guadagni, a journalist and orator of the socialists and Paul Blanshard, a very young assistant clergyman from a Congregational church. There were parades of 1800 marching the length of the main street of Plymouth. Organizers came from the American Federation of Labor, the conservative union, and the Industrial Workers of the World. The strikers listened to both, confused by the anarchists, who said that both organizations were traps for the workers, contrived by shrewd officials who wanted to live without working. Let the workers run their own strike and let those who sympathized be content to raise funds and feed the children, so thought and spoke Bartolomeo Vanzetti" (Sinclair). Finally, after a month, the factory offered a modest increase in wages, the workers accepted and returned to work.

In the novel *Boston*, Sacco, upon being sentenced for the crime he and Vanzetti were charged with committing, robbery and murder at the Slater and Morrill shoe factory in Braintree, said to the court, "I know the sentence will be between two classes, the oppressed class and the rich class, that is why I am here today on the bench, for having been of the oppressed class."

Giuseppe De Lorenzo migrated from Salina in 1900 to work for the Plymouth Cordage Company. The family started living in Duxbury in 1912. I have not found records of our great-grandfather's employment as of this writing. But we do know he had a grocery store in Quincy when Caterina, Noni and her four younger brothers came in 1912. It is unlikely working conditions were any different at the Cordage from when he was employed in 1900 and beyond.

Later, "In 1977 Massachusetts Governor Michael Dukakis issued a proclamation stating that Sacco and Vanzetti had not been treated justly and that no stigma should be associated with their names." (*Britannica Encyclopedia*)

Indeed, there was a stigma associated with being an Italian immigrant especially in the Boston area. I share this historic trial and the strike at Plymouth Cordage because my great-grandfather Giuseppe De Lorenzo was probably no longer working there, however, it gives a clear picture of the working conditions he must have endured just a few years earlier. Sinclair's novel was the most accurate research I could find at the time of this writing.

Partridge Academy

Partridge Academy, Duxbury, Mass.

Mama Caterina said, "My boys have got to get an education."

The boys graduated eighth grade from Tar Kiln School

and attended Partridge Academy in Duxbury,

the only high school in town at the time.

As teenagers they each claimed their American names

and walked almost four miles each way to school every day,

a long winter walk in the deep New England snow.

John would rather have been in the fields than in the classroom.

Joe would rather have been driving a tractor.

Bart would rather have been tinkering with an engine in the barn.

And Anthony would rather have been dreaming, drawing, and painting pictures.

But off to high school they went.

Mama Caterina said, "You must wear shirts and jackets and go to the Academy!"

Hand me Downs

Partridge Academy, 1923

The boys wore hand-me-downs:

Dress shirts, T-shirts, school jackets, but seldom ties.

Farmer boys despised wearing ties to school.

John (center back row) passed down to Joe, (photo edges torn, not seen on left).

Bartholomew is wearing only a jacket in the second row left.

Below him, Anthony is wearing just a t-shirt, seated in the front row left.

Faithful attendance and high grades, demands from Mama were eagerly met.

Demanding work was handed down, too.

Working morning to night, dawn to dusk, feeling the soil between their fingers,

Italian American work ethic handed down.

They woke up early to tend the vegetables, gather eggs, feed, and milk the horse and cows, before they walked almost four miles to high school.

Papa's humor was handed down to his boys,

laughter overflowing like bowls of blueberries in July,

made Mama Caterina smile.

Higher Education

Mama Caterina's oldest son Gaetano, now Tom, owned a store in Medford, Massachusetts.

He graduated from high school in Salina before the family immigrated to America.

John, a senior, soon attended MIT,

then transferred to the Burdette Business School in Waltham.

In a year, Joseph, who was the passionate farmer of the family,

would attend UMass Agricultural School in Amherst.

In two years, Bartholomew planned to attend MIT to study chemical engineering in Cambridge.

Anthony would start at MIT; a visual artist, he dropped out and

transferred to Antioch for Architecture.

John and Bart at MIT

John at MIT

South Shore Freight, Duxbury, MA (Courtesy of Duxbury Historical Society)

A Dowry: Linens, Copper Pots, and Land

"As recently as the 1970s, it was common practice for women in the Italian south to bring a dowry of sorts to their marriage. The bride and her family might be responsible for stocking the bedroom linens or cooking implements." (Food of the Italian South, Katie Parla)

Great-grandmother, Caterina Matarazzo, received a dowry of bedroom linens from her mother-in-law with an embroidered 'D' on it. I own an embroidered pillow cover from that collection, passed down from my grandmother to my aunt, when I was having my first child, to receive visitors and decorate my bed. I thought it odd that something so formal belonged to my peasant great-grandmother, but alas, she was no simple peasant.

I imagine my great-grandmother packing her linens and pots into a large leather cargo trunk for their passage in 1912. She was an extremely frugal woman and did not waste anything. So, her linens made their way across the pond to her new home in America. Their clothing was simple back then, so their main staples had to be linens, silverware, and copper pots. The boys had a few toys. My grandmother had a special doll. What else would they have packed but the most necessary possessions?

"Bringing a copper cookware to the marital home signaled that a woman was both a skilled cook as well as a valuable one, her worth bound to the metal from which the pots were wrought" (*Food of the Italian South*, Katie Parla). Copper and terra-cotta pots were used for cooking soups and stews, the latter called *pignate*, "used to cook octopus, goat, horse, or lamb and covered with a clay lid or sealed with bread dough, where the meat cooked for hours" (Parla).

Aunt Catherine Sangiolo once told me that she hated to eat the breakfast her grandmother prepared for her on weekend visits. She would cook the eggs and bacon together, mixed in a pot. She could not discern what was what and did not enjoy these meals. That is the way food was prepared in the old country, soups, stews, and eggs in pots, with local herbs and garden ingredients from the farm. While my Noni did not work on the farm but performed simple work in the house, her mother, my great-grandmother Caterina, did all the cooking and then went outside to begin her workday in the fields. She did not have time for fancy faire, so a slow cooking stew in a large pot for dinner or a quick morning meal of eggs and such in a small pot would suffice for her family.

Instead, my great-grandmother Caterina's noted skill, which she brought to her marriage, was in growing vegetables. I hope that when she packed for America she brought along her favorite seeds, tools, and gardening implements. There was no way to bring plants across on the ship, but if there were she would have brought her treasured malvasia grapes, wild caper plants, and fennel.

Caterina Matarazzo De Lorenzo's main marital dowry was land. In the Plymouth Land Records, the couple's first mortgage for "32 acres on 73 rods "was dated October 15th, 1914, and also was signed by Giuseppe (Joseph) and Caterina Matarazzo DeLorenzo, and she released her right to "dower" meaning "homestead." They purchased the property from Barbara Harris. She signed it as part of her dowry and marriage during that time. Women were the property of their husband until 1870 when the Married Women's Property Act was signed into law. Only married women could buy or own land in the United States from the mid-1800s, so her husband's name was also on the legal document. As late as 1950, women could not open bank accounts in their own names.

My grandmother Josephine's (Noni's) dowry might have included a sterling silver stemware set for twelve servings, a wall clock, and bed linens. My mother and father inherited the silver and the clock which passed down to the oldest son in the family. I do not know if her name was on my grandfather's business and real estate documents. The Dorchester map in this book does show that their address had "T and J Sangiolo" on it, so perhaps her name was on the mortgage for the Washington Street property at Four Corners.

A Matchmaker, Catherine 'Cay' Sangiolo

Josephine was close to her brother John.

One day, a woman named Catherine 'Cay' Sangiolo paid a visit to John's store.

He was working at the Waltham Watch Company.

John got a job there after he graduated from Burdette, repairing, and selling watches.

"Big Sis," Josephine, was in town visiting, standing quietly by the counter.

Cay met John at a social function in town for Aeolian immigrants.

Cay walked up to Josephine, looking her up and down,

and said, "Here is a pretty girl for my brother Gaetano!"

"Are we from the same town, Malfa, Salina?" Josephine asked.

"Yes, he is six years older than you, so you never went to school together," Cay replied.

Cay showed Josephine a picture of Tom with his brother Louis,

Josephine fell in love at the first sight of him,

so tall and handsome, mahogany brown eyes.

His warm smile put her heart at ease,

a promise of happiness.

Cay said, "You are as pretty as a picture!

Such milky white skin, thick curly auburn hair."

Peering through her thick eyeglasses like a fairy godmother.

A Girl for Gaetano Sangiolo

Josephine 1920, age 21

Chocolate brown eyes, four feet and ten inches,

Petite and round in all the right places,

    Josephine had several suitors.

Papa Giuseppe liked none of them for his only daughter.

John introduced Cay to Mama Caterina and Papa Giuseppe

at St. Ann's Mission Club in Watertown, Massachusetts that summer,

where island natives shared picnic gatherings at the church

and welcomed new Aeolian immigrants to Boston.

Cay made a date to visit Duxbury,

And talk further to Josephine's parents about her younger brother, Gaetano Sangiolo.

    That summer a match was made.

A Meeting with the Matchmaker

At 18, her parents agreed to a courtship for three years.

      Mama Caterina said, "You are too young,

      You will have a hard life in Boston."

Josephine was engaged to be married at 21.

Three years!

They must wait three years to marry.

Gaetano drove to Duxbury on Sundays,

his only day off.

It took him two hours driving at forty miles per hour,

to visit his future bride.

He owned a store with his brother Louis in Dorchester,

Sangiolo Brothers.

Each time he called for Josephine; brother John was their chaperone.

      Mama Caterina told John, "Never leave the young lovers alone,"

Josephine fell in love with Gaetano, over and over.

He was from the town of Capo Faro on Salina!

He was kind and gentle, and he made her laugh.

Being with him was like going home.

The Suitor, Gaetano Sangiolo

One Sunday, Gaetano told Josephine his immigrant story.

He slept under his fruit stand

on the dirty streets of New York City in 1909

He first arrived in the states at age 18.

    He said, "The living conditions for immigrants were so bad,

    that If he had the money,

    he would have gone back on the boat to Salina."

But he did not have any money,

only the clothes he wore and a will to survive.

On Salina, at Punta Scario Beach

he used to free dive for octopus, "polpo"

sold the fish for loose change to feed his family.

The Phylloxera aphid had come to Salina.

    "There was no work, we were starving,

Luigi Sangiolo, my father, was a merchant mariner," he said.

His vessel sailed no more. There was no Malvasia wine to trade

in his three-masted frigate.

The aphid had destroyed all the vineyards.

Gaetano left his verdant island for the streets paved in gold,

in America.

But America lied to him.

There were no golden streets,

only signs, everywhere in New York City,

on restaurant doors, bathroom doors,

and bar rooms:

No Italians Allowed

Italians Need NOT Apply

said the signs in store windows.

He found work selling apples, pears, oranges, and grapes on the streets,

until he and his brother Louis saved enough money

to move to Boston.

Looking in Josephine's delicate, brown eyes,

he found his home again, in America,

in Josephine.

Courtship, 1920 – 1923

Her betrothed would arrive with flowers and a bag of tangerines.

"Oh," she would say, "Thank you," as he flirted with her on walks down Lover's Lane.

Her future husband was fun-loving and jovial.

He entertained both Josephine,

and her brother John, the chaperone.

When they visited together on the farm in Duxbury,

They would stroll around the property,

traversing paths that framed the verdant vegetable fields

through the white pine grove.

Behind the high hen houses around the back,

to the side of the house where they would sit and talk under the Concord grapevines, soaking in the afternoon sun, sipping lemonade,

and eating cherries from the tree near the back porch.

Sometimes, he took her to the Boston Ballet, the opera, and the picture show.

At the opera, he always dressed in a suit and tie, black shoes, a bead of sweat on his brow.

Josephine wore one of the few white formal dresses she owned.

Brother John followed close behind, sitting between them.

He remembered the instructions from Mama Caterina,

      "Never leave them alone."

They saw *H.M.S. Pinafore,* performed by a comic opera troupe,

In the story, the captain's daughter Josephine is in love with a lower-class sailor.

They laughed and smiled at the production,

a familiar story,

Gilbert and Sullivan's fourth collaboration and first international sensation.

Brother John smiled and laughed along; he too had never seen such a thing.

It was Josephine's first time at the opera.

He spoiled her with these new experiences.

Mama Caterina said she live a charmed life, like a "principessa,"

but she knew someday they would not have time for such things.

For three years, Gaetano treated her with adventures.

A Wedding, April 9, 1923

"There is no Catholic church in Duxbury," said Papa Giuseppe.

They were married in nearby Kingston at St. Joseph's Catholic Church.

Dick, the farm horse, pulled the white-fringed buggy.

Posing for the photographer after the ceremony,

Josephine sat like a queen surrounded by her subjects.

The flower-girl sat to her right, hands folded on her lap, sad eyes, a distant stare.

Next is little Joseph Cafarella the ring bearer, wearing a white sailor shirt,

Knee shorts and white ankle socks, his elbow gently resting on the arm of her chair.

The groom, and Anthony Lopes stood behind.

Angelina Restuccia, maid of honor, sister-in-law of the matchmaker,

donned a white hat, pearls, silk dress.

Josephine wore a majestic Venetian crown that was attached to her veil.

The train hugged her elbow, trailing around the wooden chair,

a river of tulle flowing to the floor below.

She gave a knowing smile, mouth closed like her wedding party.

Perhaps smiles were not in fashion,

or the times gave nothing to smile about,

except Little Joe, his teeth show.

They waited three years for this day.

That night before undressing,

Gaetano asked Josephine if she wanted to have children.

"I think so," she answered shyly.

She had never undressed in front of anyone.

He was kind and gentle as he touched her virgin breasts.

Lover's Lane, (Courtesy of Duxbury Historical Society)

Matrimony

Maria Alaimo and Tom De Lorenzo

Joseph and Katherine De Lorenzo, Lovebirds

Tom married Maria Alaimo back in Salina.

Now, they work side by side in their neighborhood store in Medford, Massachusetts.

John married Anna Barbuto, from Somerville.

Joseph married Katherine La Greca, a neighbor from down the street.

Bart attended MIT, studied engineering, worked in New York City after graduation,

and then Ohio, where he met his wife, Gertie.

Anthony met his wife Edna in Florida after graduating from Antioch University.

John and Joe work on Sunny View Farm with Mama and Papa.

They lived in the farmhouse with their wives, Anna, and Katherine.

Mama Caterina was still in charge of the farm and her boys.

Three families under one roof.

Josephine said, "Too many breasts living in one house, cooking in one kitchen."

New Sunny View, a Poultry Farm, 1930

Tony, Tom, Bart, and John

In the 1930s, supermarkets began to open all over New England, all over the United States.

Industrial mass farming changed the agrarian way of life the De Lorenzos had come to love.

Now summer travelers use the new Route 3 to drive to the Cape.

They had to get off the highway to visit the farms in Duxbury.

Vegetable farming was a hard way to earn a living, competing with corporate farms.

The boys convinced Mama Caterina to raise chickens for meat.

Joe learned about raising poultry when he graduated from UMASS Aggy.

Now there was a new dream at Sunny View Farm,

raising and selling chickens to customers all over Boston.

While Tom and Josephine started a life together in Dorchester,

Mama, Papa (now Mom and Pop), John, and Joseph began a new venture.

Slaughtering Chickens

Joseph, Bartholomew, Mama Caterina, Josephine, Tom, John, and behind them Anthony De Lorenzo

The metal cones in the back right

were for draining the blood.

The hens were taken from the pen,

placed upside down in the cones

their heads fell below.

The men slit their throats in one cut with a sharp knife,

one carotid artery plus one jugular vein

To bleed the hen.

Then it was time to process the birds

and pluck the feathers.

Josephine and Tom's brood, the Sangiolo children, visited the farm every Sunday.

They hated their job plucking feathers.

After they were done,

Tom took them to Duxbury Beach

to play in the sand and splash in the icy, cold water.

Family Secrets

Caterina Matarazzo De Lorenzo

There was a secret about an unwed mother,

sent away to have her baby.

And one about an unfaithful lover

When her husband, dying, he lay.

There was one about a hospital,

where her son was a battle-fatigued veteran.

And one about Sunny View Farm

when a disagreement led to division.

There is at least one secret in every family

that you can't deny.

We keep old secrets close; sometimes they make us cry.

Broken hearts get beaten down,

battered now and then,

but they sit back up, brush themselves off,

and mend,

and mend.

A Letter

(from Bart in New York to Anthony in Florida, September 28, 1939)

"The office has been busy since the war broke out in Europe. Orders have come in from right and left, plenty more inquiries for us boys to work up. Things are definitely looking up and a good business boom is expected. This boom would have come war or no war. Fact is the war has tended to boom the war industries and keep others down, but they will join in the parade shortly.

You requested me to stick out my neck and make peace at the farm. Fact is, I stuck it out plenty while at the farm. It's a long story and I'll try to give you as true a picture of things as I can possibly do. On first arriving there, Mom got a hold of me and told me of my brother's plans to split. She begged me to have a talk with him and try and convince him not to do what he intended. She also wanted my honest opinion of the whole matter, and I told her that I believed it was to the best advantage of the two farms if they were run as one, mainly a true partnership. You and I had quite a talk about that when you were here.

Well, I had a talk with him on the first afternoon for about two hours long. He told me his side of the story. I advanced my arguments as to why he should not break off. I acknowledged his right to the farm, which he wanted, and informed him that mom had told all of us that the farm was to be his. He wouldn't believe me and said that he would believe it when he had the deed to the place in his own name.

Mom and Pop would "rather sell the place to a stranger than have Joe and John compete against each other." "Pop's last few days have been miserable."

But alas, that is what came to be. The house and parcels of land were divided between Joe and John, and they both were all the better for it in the end and soon after remained friends. Imagine two married couples under one roof with a mother-in-law controlling their lives? That is not a life many people would choose to live, under the best of circumstances.

Family Farm, 1939

Beloved Papa 'Pop' Giuseppe, God rest his soul, died of cancer in 1939.

No more opening the farmstand in the early morning sunshine.

No more stocking the shelves with fresh berries, tomatoes, and zucchini.

No more wars with his wife, who complained about the help, the crops needing to be picked.

When he finished the day, he would sit outside the kitchen and wait until she stopped ranting.

Giuseppe would then swing open the back screen door,

    and say, "Hello, is the war over?"

Mama 'Mom' Caterina was a tyrant and a shrewd businessperson.

She was grouchy all the time and yet, he was so funny and kind to his grandchildren.

She was in a bad car accident last year, which broke both her hands.

The doctor never straightened her fingers; she was in pain all the time.

Turkey Row

Turkey Row in Duxbury, Massachusetts began slowly. The De Lorenzo Turkey Farms made up three of the seven farms on Route 53 during the mid-1940s and 1950s when that highway was the fastest route to Cape Cod from Boston. This tourist route provided easy marketing for the seven family-owned farms selling their fresh, farm-raised turkeys for Thanksgiving dinner.

Linda De Lorenzo said, "We would get between 7,000 and 9,000 day old turkeys in the spring. We raised the poults through the summer and sold them in the fall. I remember opening day was a big day. My mother would make turkey sandwiches for the people who came to buy their turkeys. My father would tell people how to cook them for Thanksgiving. I remember a lot of people didn't know how to do it. Eventually, my father started cooking them for people, roasting them and barbecuing."

Much of what Uncle John learned came from working with other farmers and benefiting from resources offered by the state. Linda said, "There were several farms raising turkeys in Southeast Massachusetts – Middleboro, Marshfield – and the famers would get together periodically to share what worked and what didn't. The head of the Massachusetts Department of Agriculture also came to the farm to give advice. I do not remember much about the meetings except that they usually ended with a poker game. I remember sitting on my father's lap while they played cards. It was a nice group of men."

The Bongiorno family came to Duxbury in the 1930s from Quincy, Massachusetts. They opened Bongi's Turkey Farm and Store and are still in business today. John and Anna De Lorenzo remained in the turkey business until the 1970s. Uncle John taught them how to make a turkey roll.

Once the modern Route 3 to the Cape was complete, the turkey farm business began to ebb slowly. Along with the advent of refrigerated trucks, tourists now bought their turkeys in local supermarkets.

The Original John De Lorenzo Turkey Farm

established 1946

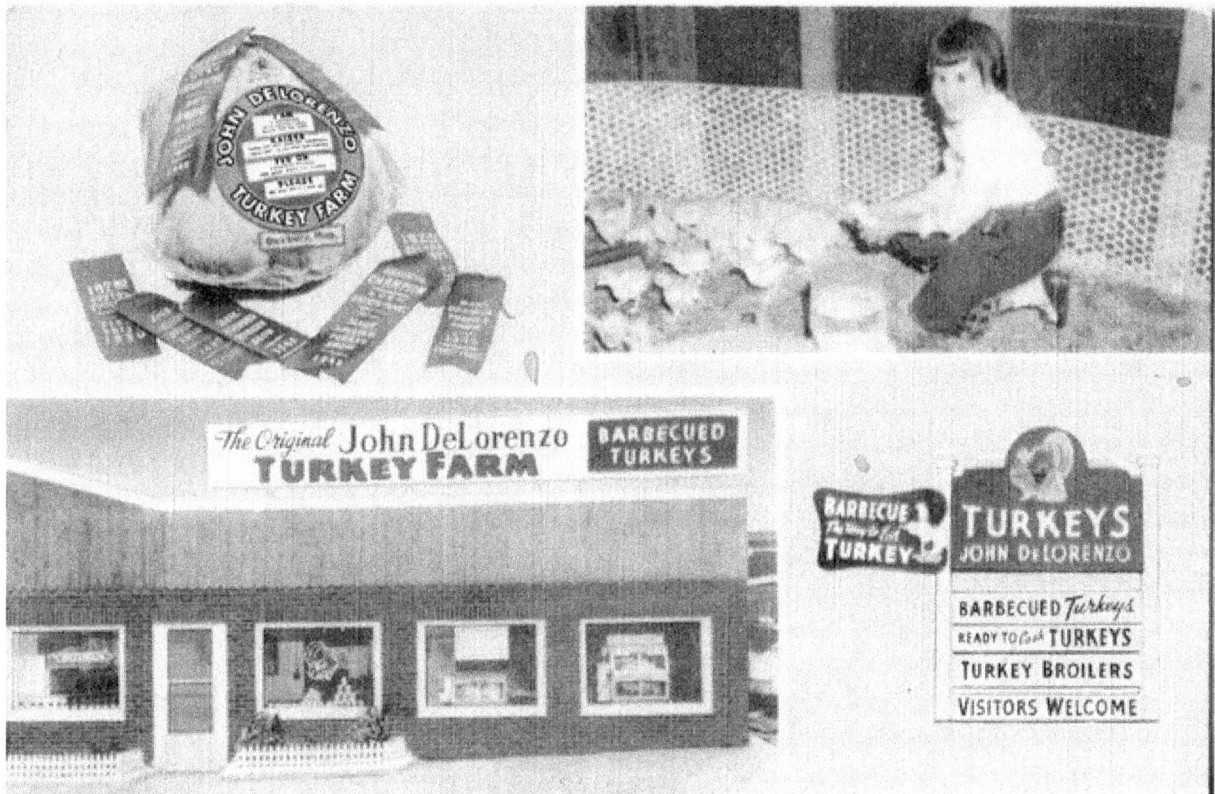

First, John raised chickens for six years or so.

Then he learned how to make a turkey roll

from Edwards Farm in Stoughton, Massachusetts.

His sons, John David Jr. and Joseph, hauled 50-pound bags of feed each morning to the barns.

"My mom Anna and Nona Caterina wore white gloves and fancy hats to the Grand Opening

Of the John De Lorenzo Turkey Farm," said Linda De Lorenzo.

John's baby girl, Catherine, aka Sassy, was the poster girl.

Big sister Linda nicknamed her Sassy because she could not pronounce Cathy.

Sassy was born the year they started the award-winning Turkey Farm on Turkey Row.

Under the watchful eye of Mama Caterina,

Anna kept a farm ledger of all expenses; she was not good with numbers.

If Anna purchased something deemed unnecessary from her mother-in-law,

their pay was docked that amount the following week.

Piles of farm ledgers littered one of the upstairs bedrooms in later years.

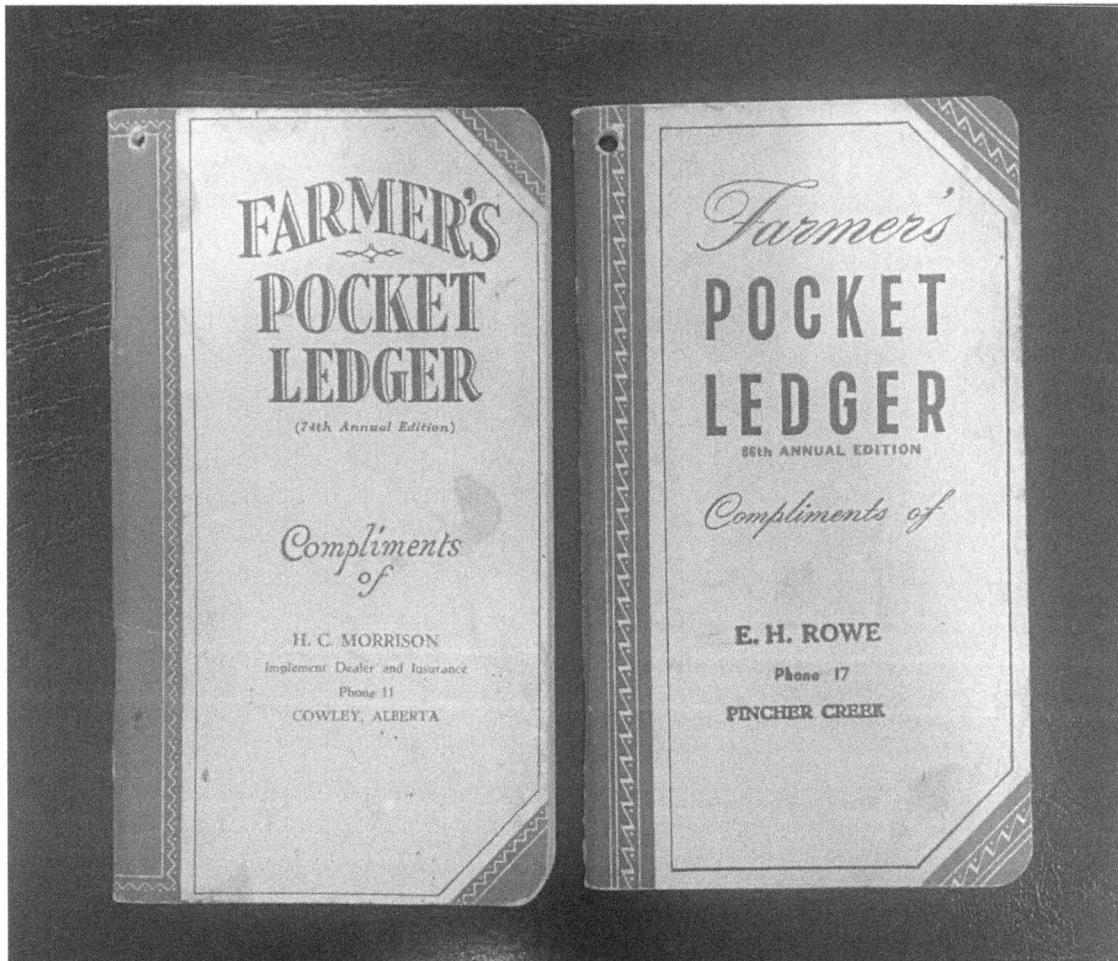

Farm Ledger (1916 example)

Dec 1   Eggs sold to Bertha Patter $1.00

3   "   "   "Elmer Hogel 2 doz, $1.20

"   Eggs gave to Elsie Brown, .60

6   *52 ½ dozen eggs @.55 Crosby Bros Co $28.86*

Joseph De Lorenzo's Turkeys and Cranberries

Cranberry Growers Magazine interviewed Joseph De Lorenzo.

"The only one of the six siblings to remain in farming,

Joseph always enjoyed growing things, his vocation, avocation, and plain old pleasure.

He loved learning about how to grow,

evidenced by the trellised roses round his front doorway,

a grape arbor, peaches, plums, cherries,

nectarines, strawberries, and raspberries.

He and Kay built their home and their life with their bare hands.

A graduate of the University of Massachusetts Agricultural College" (Cranberry Growers).

First, they raised chickens.

There were woods to clear, and poultry shelters to erect on the land

given to them by Mama Caterina and Papa Giuseppe.

They began with nine 20 x 40 buildings.

Five years later, they had three buildings four hundred feet in length housing 25,000 broilers.

It was good for several years; then they had trouble making ends meet.

They gave up the chickens and turned to turkeys.

He and his wife Katherine 'Kay' put up the barn.

They remained in the turkey business for six years; around 1947 they gave it up.

In the meantime, he had been building cranberry bogs, by hand.

When he switched to cranberrying, he had but 8 acres.

Later he had about two hundred acres and joined the Ocean Spray Cooperative.

His oldest son Joseph ran the bogs.

Joseph senior pitched in around harvest time. Katherine assisted.

Joseph loved cranberry harvest time. He liked getting into the bogs.

He even operated the walking water reel.

He would laugh, "When it gets to be October, it starts getting cold.

Especially when you fall into a ditch, and you have to empty your boots."

Nobody knew better that turkey and cranberries go together.

He raised them both.

Joseph De Lorenzo, age 75, Cranberry Growers Magazine

Anthony and Edna, 1947

Minesweeper on Duxbury Beach

The Coast Guard sold off surplus materials at the end of WWII.

This inspired the youngest brother Anthony to purchase a 72-foot yacht

For pennies on the dollar.

Sailed it to Florida where he met his bride Edna in 1947.

After the war, Mama convinced her youngest son Anthony to return to Duxbury, again,

this time offering a house and land.

Joe and Kay had moved down the road,

built a new home on De Lorenzo Drive.

Tony and Edna moved into Joe's old house and opened their own poultry farm.

Mama Caterina never wanted her three boys competing for customers on the same road.

Work

Hard work and keeping busy were ingrained in me as a young child. Dad was the first son of Italian immigrants. My grandfather Nonno Gaetano got a loan to buy the building that housed their home and store. Those assets, along with renting rooms on the third floor of their Dorchester home, a former commercial office building, helped the family survive the Great Depression. They ate fresh fruit and produce from the store when most people were starving. Nonno was a good businessperson and they prospered during and after World War II.

But their life was the store.

Sangiolo Brothers grocery became Sangiolo and Sons when my paternal grandfather's brother Louis passed away in the 1920s from a disease he acquired during WWI.

All five Sangiolo children worked at the store. Mary was the bookkeeper. Lou and Joe serviced the customers by weighing pasta and delivering orders. Catherine and Tom worked in the store when they were young adolescents. Lou and Joe looked forward to a five-cent tip or, if they were lucky, ten cents. Nonno did not like spending money. When Joe suggested that they sell meat like the neighboring Greeks, Nonno said, "No, then we will have to buy a freezer, and that is too expensive." Joe explained how they could expand the business to make more money. The answer was always "No." "But why Dad?" asked young Joe. "Because I said so," he would reply, the famous last words all Sangiolo children heard.

Work, working all day, was the Sangiolo way. You had to maximize every minute of each hour and get the honey-do list done. From the time he woke on weekends until about three in the afternoon, my father Louis worked in his woodshop building kitchen cabinets and bathroom vanities in addition to his full-time career in manufacturing at GTE Sylvania. He named his side business Esten Cabinets. We lived on the corner of Esten Road and Atkinson Avenue. Esten was a decorated veteran from World War II who was from Stoughton, my hometown. As children, we were not aware that our father was a World War II veteran.

I woke to the smell of sawdust and the sound of the table saw beneath my bedroom which was directly above the garage and points north of Dad's first shop. It was not until little brother Carl began digging holes under the screen porch with his Tonka trucks that my father had the idea to dig a foundation and move his shop underneath what later became a four-season room. Luckily, that was around the time I moved to the pink shag bedroom downstairs and could finally sleep late on weekends during my high school years. Dad would end his workday with a shot and a beer and then take a nap. He was a good role model for napping. I still end my workday with a fifteen to twenty-minute nap on the couch after school. I have Dad to thank for this after-work recumbent constitutional.

Having grown up in a small family business, it is no wonder my father was skeptical about my choice of marriage. My husband owned a small local restaurant at the time of our engagement. Dad was proud of Barry when he opened the second restaurant, 85 Main. Now he owns a restaurant group, Green Valley Hospitality, and four themed restaurants all in Northeastern Connecticut which provide a wonderfully comfortable life for our family, but does it come at a cost? The restaurants are not in our backyard, well not anymore. We lived next door to the cafe for two and half years until we bought our home on twenty acres of land when our first child was a toddler.

Our family room houses a computer networked to all four restaurants. Every morning, my husband, a good businessperson, gets up and looks at all the reports from the previous night's numbers. Work, his work, exists in our home and is always calling, texting, and working its way into our dinner conversations.

Our life is the store.

I am guilty as well, of bringing my work into our home. For twenty years I was a singer-songwriter with my sound equipment and instruments in the living room. I wrote songs in journals at the kitchen table when our kids were young. Now, I am on spring break, two weeks off from my work at a middle boarding school and here I sit working at the computer on this essay.

The innate drive to work, create, and stay busy all stems from a pattern, a worry, and a need for survival. The glass was always half empty. There was never enough in a home with five children and unbeknownst to us, they were always just squeaking by each month. Dad's side job helped my parents stay afloat financially. Children of the Great Depression, my parents both scrimped and saved everything. You never threw anything away. Dad reused wood from old jobs to build my mother's furniture or to fix something that needed mending. He reused nails, screws, and pieces of Formica to make me a corner desk in my childhood bedroom and later to re-laminate an old children's table for my kids, the same Formica first used over thirty years before.

We fill the cabinets in our laundry room with scraps and pieces of odd things like wine corks and ribbon in a craft closet. There is a battery basket, bird basket, cat basket, and laundry cleaner shelf. Everything has a purpose, and most things get recycled, re-used, or donated.

Why do we work? For whom are we working? Our children, their children, our retirement, and our country. Or do we just love to work to create something beautiful? Someone recently shared the title of a new book, *Rest is Resistance by Tricia Hersey.* Perhaps I should take a nap instead of writing this essay.

Hand drawn map by Louis Sangiolo

Chapter Four: The Grocery at Dorchester Four Corners, 1923 – 1952

Sangiolo and Sons was located on the corner of 356 Washington Street in Dorchester, in the middle of Dakota and Bowdoin Street, an area known as Dorchester Four Corners. My paternal grandfather, Tom 'Gaetano' Sangiolo, opened a small grocery with his brother Louis called *Sangiolo Bros* soon after he arrived in Boston in his twenties. He left Salina by himself at the age of eighteen in 1909 with nothing but the shirt on his back.

His sister Cay (Catherine) had come to the United States before him and was living in New York City, New York. She moved to Dorchester first and opened a store with her husband Anthony Restuccia.

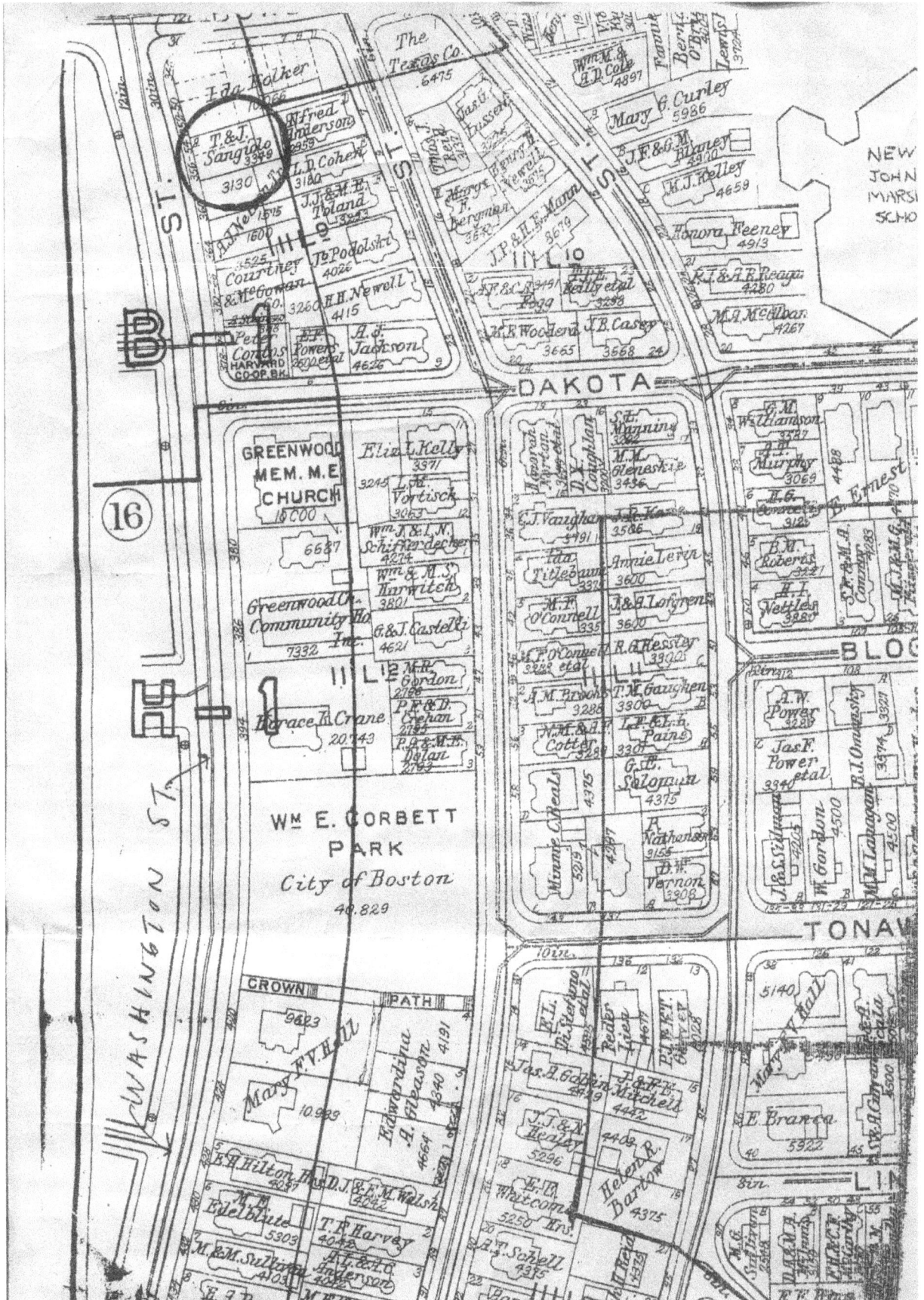

Sangiolo Bros.

A postcard sent home to Salina, 1909

Sisters Giannina and Caterina (Cay) Sangiolo and their mother, center, Maria Cafarella

Gaetano and Luigi, (Tom and Louis),

young, ambitious immigrant siblings

were partners in business.

Keys hung from Luigi's waist,

jingle, jingle, jangled every morning,

as he unlocked the storefront grate.

Tom drove to the market to buy fresh fruits and vegetables, scrutinizing them for freshness.

Everyone loved gregarious Gaetano. All his *'compare'*,

men peddling and working at Boston's wholesale fruit and vegetable market,

greeted him with big smiles, handshakes, and cigars.

Tom hand-picked his produce, then hurried back to the store to his eager customers.

Wife

La Cucina Piccola fa la Case Grande

'A little kitchen makes a large house.' Josephine Sangiolo

His young bride, Josephine, had her place in the store.

Together they greeted customers, filled orders in brown paper bags,

And conversed with their neighbors who patronized the business.

Growing up on a farm, she had no sense in the esoteric of life at all, no fancy decor.

They worked together to take care of their future.

Boston was a crowded, dirty, noisy place

but she did not mind, she was a pragmatic woman.

Dirty dishes could wait, the dust would be there tomorrow.

She spent her days working by her husband's side.

This was her new life.

The two were frugal, industrious immigrants,

but they made work fun.

Dorchester had lively neighborhoods.

The Greek neighbors sold meat,

Down the street was the Five-and-Dime whose windows displayed toys and magazines.

There was a bank and the family doctor on Upham's Corner,

and each parish had its own church.

The YMCA was housed in a community center one block away.

Mother's Rest, a park, was the place to walk her first baby Mary.

My Little Josephine

Josephine, Mary, and Gaetano

Gaetano smiled proudly at Josephine with a twinkle in his eye,

When he called her to his side, he would say,

      "My little Giuseppina"

to his young bride.

Louis and Margaret lived upstairs.

They shared their first home with them on Westville Street.

Louis was sick from the First World War.

Margaret was a young widow when he died.

Josephine loved Margaret and held her when she cried.

Sangiolo and Sons, Dorchester Four Corners

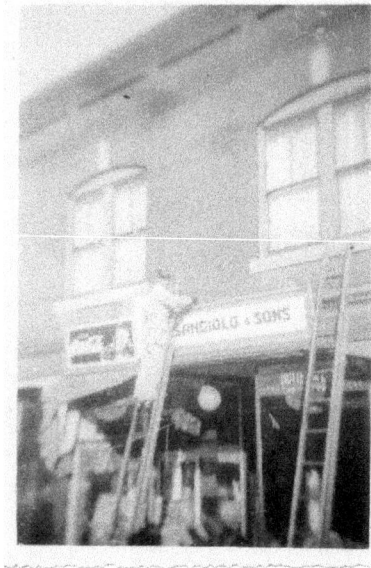

Gaetano changed the name of the store to Sangiolo and Sons.

Now he was in business with his children.

Josephine had customers to greet, laundry to hang, meals to cook and eat.

On either side of the promenade, trees lined Washington Street.

Streetcars passed by, filling their home with dust,

white soot coated the living room windows.

She did not mind the dirt.

She would say, "It will still be there tomorrow."

She was a city girl now, no more princess life on the country farm.

Now Josephine decided how she spent her time,

No more Mama Caterina to mind.

Walking up and down the stairs

from the store to their home,

"Ba dum, bad dum, ba dum dum dum," her daily exercise.

Baby Mary

Mary – 1924

Their first baby was a girl, beautiful Mary.

     "Tutta mia," her first words, meant "all mine, all mine."

A beautiful, brown-eyed toddler

with a young mind

all her own,

Josephine could not get her first daughter to listen at all!

Valentine

February fourteen, 1926

Gaetano shoveled coal into the furnace all through the night,

during a terrible winter storm,

awaiting the birth of their second child.

Thank God the coal man came that day,

poured bags of black chips down the chute into the basement.

Gaetano turned over the red-hot embers as the snow kept falling, falling,

keeping his young bride warm,

while she labored into the wee hours of the morning,

until she delivered Louis, a valentine.

Mr. Di Giacomo

First, they lived in an apartment on Westville Street

downstairs from Mr. Di Giacomo who had two sons, Fred, and Louis.

Fred became a doctor, the Sangiolo family practitioner in Upham's Corner.

The week Uncle Louis Sangiolo died,

Gaetano and Josephine took little Mary to the funeral.

They left their son, three-year-old Louis, with their neighbor, Mr. Di Giacomo.

Little Louis asked the man working on his porch, "What are you doing?"

As the man cut a jigsaw puzzle out of plywood,

he asked little Louis, "Do you want to try?"

"Yes," he replied.

Louis began playing with wood in the back room of the store,

old pieces of peach baskets, wooden crates,

and whatever else he could find.

Playing with scraps of wood to pass the time,

while his parents worked all day.

Louis built things out of wood

      ever since the day

he learned

      how to cut a jigsaw puzzle with Mr. Di Giacomo.

Second Son Joseph

Louis, baby Joseph and Mary

Joseph was born in early June,

springtime,

Josephine's second baby boy.

Mama's pride and joy.

"Giuseppe, sensa niente paura!'"

Joseph has no fear!

He made her crazy,

climbing all over the place,

table, chairs, stairs to the store.

A little boy with a curious mind.

The Great Depression

During the Great Depression, Gaetano secured a bank loan

to purchase the commercial property that housed his business.

The building was once a motor garage

that stored automobiles for residents without personal carriage houses.

The Sangiolo family moved in to the second floor.

Metal wheels squealed across the trolley tracks outside their door.

White noise, the din of the city, a cacophony of background music.

Their new neighborhood was a melting block of nations,

Italians, Polish, Irish, German, Jews, and Christians,

living beside one another in brownstones and vacated commercial lots.

Life in Boston *was the store*, open seven days a week.

Natali Brandy, Pa's helper, lived with them in a room on the second floor.

He opened the shop on Sunday when the family went to Duxbury.

Brandy minded the place on weekdays

while Tom went to the market for produce daily.

He bought bulk pasta from the Marchetti Family

who later opened Prince Macaroni in the North End.

Gaetano and Josephine, Italian American parents,

Learned to speak English at home to their children.

Only when they had private conversations did they speak in Italian to each other.

The children were American and soon, Gaetano naturalized to become a citizen in 1934,

and much later Josephine did the same in 1943.

The young couple made their work a game with a lot of love, food, and laughter.

Gaetano changed his name to Tom. He entertained the customers, in Yiddish.

He would say, "Pick up your dress pretty girl."

They would smile and say, "Oh Tom!"

Mary learned to keep the ledger books in the big rolltop desk in the back of the store.

Sons, Louis and Joseph, helped in front serving customers,

stocking shelves with canned goods and dry groceries,

and delivering orders for a nickel tip, sometimes a dime.

They packed those orders in three peach baskets lined up in a pushcart.

The boys had to get up early on Saturday, reluctantly, to do their chores.

"Oh Pa, do we have to?" asked Joe.

Lou the oldest, always said, "Sure Pa."

The boys "Competed for tips, competed for everything, two years apart, Mama Mia!"
said Ma.

They attended John Marshall School and then English High School,

had to bring home high grades on their report cards.

Later, the two girls went to Jeremiah Burke High School, a secretarial school.

Mary liked to go on adventures with her friends.

Little Catherine had to stay at home and help Joe in the store.

For fun, Joe would reach for a roll of toilet paper for a customer,

and say, "See this, this is the best toilet paper in the world,

If you get any scratches, you bring it back and I will fully guarantee your satisfaction!"

A tease just like his father, Catherine just laughed and laughed.

Popeye, Pa's hunting dog

lived outside in his doghouse where animals belonged.

"No animals allowed in the home,

animals belong in a barn," Josephine would say to her children.

When the store mouser called "The Cat" was ready to deliver a new litter of kittens,

the pregnant tabby would come to find Tom.

"Meow, meow, purr, purr, purr,"

Scratching on his pant leg.

Tom would make her a bed in a cardboard box lined with a potato sack.

He always gave the baby kittens away to customers.

Young Catherine used to play with The Cat like a doll,

dressed her up in baby clothes and put her in the perambulator.

The Carpenters

Doris Carpenter

The newly purchased commercial building on Washington Street.

housed the store, a retail bakery, and three apartments,

making a home for the Sangiolo family during very uncertain times.

It was the Great Depression.

During those years, they rented the third-floor rooms to Tony and Doris Carpenter.

The Sangiolo family and Natali Brandy occupied the first and second floors.

Nicolas (Natalie) Brandy

Sept / 939

Natalie Brandy and Gaetano Sangiolo

Aunt Mary said, "Pa paid him in addition to his room and board. He used to watch the store until closing time until he died. The store was open seven days a week. After Brandy died Pa closed the store at 1 pm on Sundays."

Uncle Lou said, "When Mr. Brandy was alive, going to Duxbury was a ritual. The Sangiolo family went there every Sunday. The uncles at home at the time were Uncle John and Uncle Joe and Uncle Tony until he moved to Florida."

Natalie Brandy dressed in black jacket and white-collared shirt,

a smile on his face, happy to be at work.

Greeted the customers with his thick Italian accent.

Stood proudly by the produce,

colorfully displayed outside the front door.

Packed bulk pasta as he counted the coins,

after doing his math on a paper bag.

Leaned over the counter chewing tobacco, then he rose and

followed the ladies to the door to thank them.

Spewed his chew six feet across the street.

He lived upstairs in the back room

on the second floor, above the store,

a place of his own to rest and sleep.

Garbage Man, Ice Man, Knife Man, Milk Man

Everyone on the block had a huge garbage pan in the ground.

Weekly, the Garbage Man came around,

pulled the pan up and out

emptied the stench into his truck,

sweet smell of refuse.

The Ice Man came around too,

delivering blocks of ice

for the Ice Box

to keep perishable cold food.

The Knife Man,

sharpened knives

for the people of Dorchester.

The Milk Man

delivered fresh milk daily

in cases of glass bottles.

These were all important jobs in the early 20th century.

The Spartans

In the early summer of 1937

a group of boys met in a room on the second floor,

of the Greenwood Community Center on Washington Street.

They formed an athletic club at the Dorchester YMCA.

Their leader was named Neil Craig, but the team needed a name.

On the wall of the room was a map of Ancient Europe and the Near East.

One of the boys noticed the location of Sparta and suggested their name be The Spartans.

It was voted on and adopted unanimously.

Those in attendance were Rich Smith, Ed Garro, Lou Sullivan, Alan Sternfield, Herb Vortisch, Fran Earley, and Lou Sangiolo.

Prior to World War II, new members joined the team: Bill and Dick Shea, Joe Sangiolo, Charlie Kurker, Fred Willett, Joe McNamara, Archie White, Bob Mahoney, Jack White, Ray Campbell, and Ed Tamoush.

The boys played basketball,

uniforms and everything,

and softball on Y-Land,

a turn-around track loop for the streetcars of the Boston Elevated.

They played baseball on a sand lot at Mother's Rest.

Lou and Joe built a hut in the backyard,

behind the store,

out of scraps of wood, slats of peach baskets.

In the evenings, they hit bottle stoppers with the store broom.

Batting practice against the brick wall out back

preparing for their games

with the Spartans.

Catherine, Their Baby Girl

Josephine and baby Catherine

Catherine was born in a small, private hospital nearby.

Tom brought Little Lou to see his new sister.

He saw the jaundiced baby with black hair, and said, "Mama why did you buy a dark baby?"

She needed to be placed in a sunny window.

Catherine had a full crop of dark hair and very dark skin.

Little Lou was happy that her skin got lighter after she came home with Mama.

A Visit from Maria Cafarella Sangiolo, Nonna Sangiolo

Nonna Cafarella and Louis 1920

Maria Cafarella Sangiolo lost her husband, Luigi Sangiolo,

on 27 August 1919 in Capo Faro, Salina.

Nonna left the island to reunite with her children in America.

Taking turns, she spent months at a time at her daughters Cay and Jennie's home,

and she stayed with the Sangiolo family in Dorchester.

Tom and Josephine spoke Italian to his mother for she could not speak English.

Nonna Maria loved the children and especially loved to play with baby Catherine.

She was a fun, loving grandmother.

Prayed to the Blessed Virgin daily with her Rosary beads.

Taught the grandchildren to speak Italian, tall and warm and loving, like her son Tom.

Piano Lesson for Catherine Sangiolo

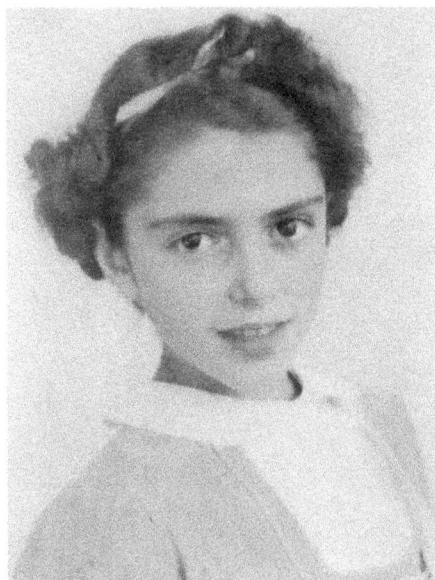

Young Catherine Sangiolo

Catherine's best friend, Virginia Moran, had a piano.

Virginia loved to play.

At nine years old, Catherine wanted to learn how to play just like her friend.

Gaetano bought her a piano but would not pay for lessons.

Catherine rang her cousin in West Medford, Catherine De Lorenzo, who played the instrument.

She and her big sister Mary took the train to Medford, to learn how to play from their cousin,

together.

Young Catherine Sangiolo loved the instrument more than Mary.

Catherine played all the time.

Catherine wanted to become a musician.

> Her father said, "I love when you play the piano Catherine,
>
> it fills our home with music."

Teenage Beauty

Tom watched little Catherine like a hawk.

He knew the dangers of men and pretty women.

Catherine had curfews and limits.

He did not let her out of his sight.

Pure Italian, olive-skinned, brown-eyed beauty with perfect curves,

she went off to the Fireman's Ball for her first date of dancing at age 16,

unbeknownst to her father.

"Be home before your father," Josephine said biting her hand, "Mama Mia!"

All night, Josephine waited at the top of the stairs for Catherine to return,

Nine o'clock, nine-thirty, ten o'clock.

Then she heard her daughter's delicate feet hop, hop, hop, up the landing outside.

And while praying the Rosary, "Hail Holy Queen, finally," she said to herself,

     "She is home before my husband!"

Josephine heard the door handle turn; up the flight of stairs came her daughter,

dancing a jitterbug two-step swing, just as Gaetano closed the store door downstairs.

Catherine flew to the second floor, just in time.

Hands on her hips, "Madonna!" Josephine cried, biting her hand, "Mama Mia!

You made it home before your father!"

The Birds and the Bees

Josephine and her husband worried about their beautiful daughter Catherine.

Talking to girls about sex was forbidden in those days.

The Sangiolos were Catholic and believed in the Immaculate Conception

but knew the dangers of relationships between young girls and boys.

A customer of the store was always bragging about her beautiful daughter

whose name was Peg.

She was "so beautiful, very smart and had many callers," said Peg's mother.

Josephine soon learned that Peg was pregnant.

One day, she told Catherine what had happened to Peg and said,

"She is being sent away to live with the nuns.

She will never see her parents,

or friends, family, or baby.

 Ever again!"

That was the way Catherine learned about the birds and the bees.

Josephine put the fear of God into her daughter, forever.

A practical mother, she solved that problem in one conversation.

Baby Tom

Josephine gave birth to baby Tom at age forty-one.

He is seven years younger than Catherine.

Pa's pride and joy,

just like his father:

thoughtful, funny, smart,

dark and handsome.

Walks like him, sits with his hands on his belly just like his father.

Laughs like his father.

Louis carried his chubby baby brother up the stairs on Sundays

after the family's weekly visit to Duxbury.

He trudged slowly from the beach and sun and the weight of the baby boy.

Louis built him a wooden rocking duck in his woodworking class

at Oliver Wendell Holmes School.

The Sangiolo Family: Josephine, Mary, Joseph, Catherine, Louis, Young Tom and Gaetano (Tom)

Saturday Morning

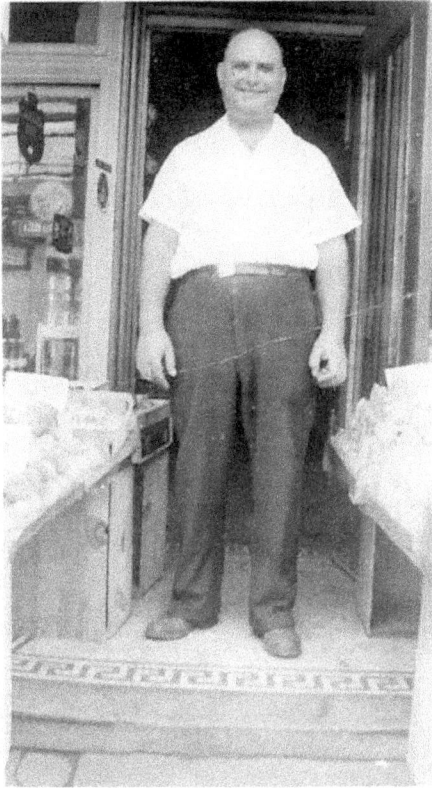

Gaetano (Tom) Sangiolo

The boys worked in the store on Saturday mornings

when they began attending John Marshall Middle School.

Jingle, jangle, jangle, jingle, jangle, gee,

sang Pa's keys,

hanging from the belt loop of his slacks,

an apron tied around his back.

He would unlock the gate, pull down the awning in the early morning.

"Pa, do we have to work?" whined Joe.

Lou minded his father, got the pushcart ready to load the orders.

Joe carried bags in his hands, bags bigger than him.

Pa went to market three times a week in his Plymouth Woody Station Wagon

to purchase fresh produce.

"Lou and Joe, stock the fruit outside on the stand.

Don't bruise the pears, neatly display the fresh strawberries,

Arrange the cherries, peaches, and plums like a rainbow," said their father.

Tom took great pride in his work

and in his sons.

Josephine baked pies

when the fruit became overripe.

Food was never wasted.

They sold fresh bread and fresh milk delivered by the milkman,

kept everything cool in the ice box.

Later in the day, Gaetano sat at the big rolltop desk,

taught Mary how to settle customer accounts.

During the Depression he sold on credit,

wrote the prices out on paper bags.

Customers did not always have cash.

They would smile and say, "Thank you, Tom."

He helped them out like a good neighbor.

Sundays

The Sangiolo family visited Duxbury,

every Sunday, no matter the weather:

summer heat, spring rain, cool autumn days, winter snow.

The children loved going to the farm,

played with their uncles,

drove Grandma Caterina crazy with their constant cackling.

Joe loved to sing Sinatra, "All or Nothing at All," with a broom for a mike,

the girls screamed with delight.

Grandma Caterina did not have the patience or time for grandchildren.

Times were hard on the farm, growing fruit and veggies, raising chickens.

She always had work, work, work to be done.

There was never a moment to sit and visit.

The children were afraid of their grandmother on the farm.

Grandma Caterina was mean and told them to go outside and play. "Shoo, shoo," she'd say.

Shortly after they arrived, they would beg their Pa to take them to the beach.

He never said no.

Purple Feet

Josephine, Mary, Pa (Tom), Joe and Louis

Una cattiva non fa buon vino!

"You can't make good wine from bad grapes." Josephine Sangiolo

"Stomping grapes is the best way to make wine,

we did it to pass the time," explained Josephine.

She loved stomping Malvasia grapes as a child in Malfa.

Her feet were yellow for two weeks, but she did not mind.

"Let's make Duxbury Red, the uncle's wine!" said Lou and Joe.

In late September, when nights were cool, Lou and Joe helped Uncle John harvest the fruit.

They picked the concord grapes at night; that's how John got the deep red color.

With the old truck, they would pick up a 32- pound crate of elegante and zinfandel grapes nearby.

The next morning, they would unload them into the cellar,

pour all the grapes into a big metal vat,

use a hand crank to loosen grapes from the stem.

The boys took off their shoes and pressed gently to extract the juice with their feet,

dirty and dry, stained for weeks, but they did not mind.

They gently pressed the purple balls with their toes.

Pressing with their feet started the fermentation,

no worries about dirt in the formation,

strained out the germs with the skin, pulp, seeds, and stems,

months of curing got rid of them.

Uncle John poured the juice into the old oak barrel out back,

Placed the cover tightly on top to rest. Months of curing finished Uncle John's wine.

His daughters, Linda and Sass, were the only two girls in Duxbury who knew how to tap a keg!

The extended family met at summer picnics, Christmas, and weddings,

Where we often shared a bottle of Duxbury Red.

Uncle Tom's 'Woody' Ford Wagon by Linda De Lorenzo

Gaetano Sangiolo, Uncle Tom, scraping his wooden wagon.

"Almost every Sunday morning

I would wake and peer out my bedroom window at the wooden station wagon below,"

said Linda De Lorenzo.

 "It was like Christmas on Sunday every week!

Uncle Tom always brought bags of fruit and treats -

paper bags of fruit and candy filled to the brim for me."

On some Sundays the De Lorenzos would go to the city,

to visit Uncle Tom and Aunt Josephine.

"I would sit under the skylight in Aunt Josephine's kitchen in Dorchester,

looking up at the light, basking in the sunshine,

and wonder how that sun got up there?

In the middle of the city in a dark, dirty neighborhood."

Mother's Rest

1932

Louis & Joe

Louis and Joseph Sangiolo

When it was time to take her fifth child, baby Tom, outside,

Josephine took him for a walk in the perambulator

past the church, past Dakota Street

To Mother's Rest, on the same side of the street as Sangiolo and Sons,

a lovely park for the people in the neighborhood.

With a long bench at the top, she had an expansive view of the city.

The boys enjoyed sledding in winter.

She sat with baby Tom and visited with the other moms.

Lou and Joe played baseball at the bottom of the hill in spring.

Spaghetti and Meatballs

On Sunday mornings, Tom used every pot

in Josephine's kitchen to make dinner.

      It was his time to shine.

He cooked all morning, waking at dawn to sauté' the garlic,

simmer the onions, crush the tomatoes,

      to make spaghetti sauce for the family.

He would mix meatballs from scratch

using ground beef, ground veal,

parsley, breadcrumbs, one egg,

and freshly grated parmesan cheese.

Baked the meatballs in the oven,

placed them lovingly in his sauce to simmer all morning.

      When it was time to eat, he would walk down the creaky old stairs

from the apartment, twenty steps down to the store,

and fill a paper bag with two pounds of bulk spaghetti.

He boiled the pasta,

and served up spaghetti and meatballs for Sunday dinner.

      He and Josephine shared a pound of pasta between them.

The second pound was for the kids to share.

      Tom made such a mess in the kitchen, using every utensil, every pot.

Josephine did not mind, the house smelled of meatballs and sauce.

      He filled their home with his love for food.

Summer Vacation

Back: Lou, Mary, Joe

Front: Josephine, baby Tom, Gaetano, and Catherine Sangiolo

When Lou was about ten, they sent him away

to Sunny View Farm for two weeks each summer.

Plucking chicken feathers, collecting eggs from the hens,

      he would complain, "The hens peck at my fingers when I try to reach each egg!"

The uncles would laugh at him as he ran out and cried.

He did whatever job his Nonna Caterina assigned.

He learned to drive on the old farm tractor.

During the Great Depression,

They needed every hand on the farm.

He wanted to stay in Dorchester, play baseball and basketball at the Y,

With his friends, The Spartans,

but every summer they sent him and said, "This is your vacation."

To young Louis, it never felt like a vacation.

His brother Joe was jealous,

because Louis got to spend the summer near the beach, on the farm.

But Lou told his brother it was "no picnic,"

and Nonna Caterina was tough.

He said, "She ruled the farm with her iron fist."

The grand piano still stood in the living room, but no one ever played it.

Josephine, A Working Mother

Even after Black Thursday on October 24, 1929,

the Sangiolo family always had good food to eat from the store,

and the family farm in Duxbury.

Josephine loved being a mother and she loved working in the store.

Josephine in front of Sangiolo and Sons

Some days, she missed Duxbury.

So, she planted flower boxes of pink petunias

and periwinkle blue morning glories that climbed up the fire escape.

When there was work to be done, she tied baby Tom to the fire escape,

so he could get some fresh air and not wander in the neighborhood.

How else could she watch him while she worked in the store?

The back yard was lined with lilac trees.

Tom planted tomatoes every summer.

And this year, he planted two new peach trees.

Italian Festival

One day, young Catherine and Josephine went to a church festival.

Josephine nudged her daughter to look across the way, with disapproval.

The Sangiolo girls dressed properly, in clean dresses.

A woman should be ladylike in public.

There was a young attendant sitting,

privately, quietly at the entrance.

Josephine whispered to Catherine,

      "Look at that woman's legs so wide apart.

That is terrible, you can see her crow's nest!"

Catherine tried hard not to laugh.

Josephine said, "She knows how to cook the Puttanesca, the whore's meal.

She throws everything she finds in the cupboard to make the sauce quickly,

then gets back to her work!"

Recipe for Puttanesca Sauce

Boil salted water.

Sweat garlic and aromatics: anchovies, chopped black olives, capers, Calabrian chili, and sauté for a couple of minutes.

Add tomatoes, whatever you have in the pantry, but pureed San Marzano are best.

Cook the pasta for 30 seconds to a minute, less than the box recommends.

Reserve a cup of water for the next steps.

Combine pasta and sauce and ¼ cup of reserved water.

Cook for an additional 2 minutes, until pasta is al dente, and the sauce has reduced to coat each noodle.

Add parmesan cheese and dried basil, chopped parsley.

Serve!

Christmas

Snow covered the dirt and grime of the city streets.

Pa would drag the last fir tree from the store up the stairs on Christmas Eve.

When the children were asleep,

he and Josephine would decorate the tree

until the wee hours of the morning.

Santa's gift.

    The children hung stockings for small treats.

Christmas dinner lasted all day,

as the family feasted on a Sunny View farm turkey,

chicken soup with meatballs,

bulk spaghetti from the store,

and fresh squash and beans.

    There were few gifts at Christmas,

but the Sangiolo family always shared a delicious, big meal.

Ice Skates

Louis and Joe

worked in the family store after school and

early on Saturday mornings.

They earned a nickel, a dime,

each time they delivered groceries.

Louis was saving his loose change

to buy a pair of ice skates.

He saw them in the window at the Five-and-Dime.

Pa did not know how to skate.

He asked Lou,

"What do you need ice skates for?

Save your money!"

Pa worked every day.

He did not have much time to play, except on Sundays.

Secretly,

Lou bought that pair of ice skates,

and hid them in the basement,

near the furnace so that Pa

would never know how he spent

his tips and savings on a pair of ice skates.

World War II

John, Joseph, and Bart DeLorenzo were essential workers and avoided the draft.

Anthony returned to Duxbury to work for the Coast Guard.

Three family sons survived the war.

Joseph Cafarella, Josephine's ring bearer,

son of Frank and Jenny Sangiolo Cafarella

served in the Army Air Corps as a pilot and returned home to become a doctor.

Alfred Restuccia, the matchmaker's son,

son of Anthony and Cay Restuccia

served in the Army Air Corps and

returned to work in the family story in Medford.

Louis Sangiolo, my father, the youngest to serve,

signed up at 18 and left MIT after a year in the accelerated program.

He wanted to be a pilot,

but the Army Air Corps had enough pilots.

He trained to be a gunner.

After 25 missions in the belly of a B-24, he returned home, a different person.

Played baseball, had three girlfriends, and returned to MIT too soon,

but he flunked out, he could not focus on his studies, he was suffering from battle fatigue.

Aunt Cay, the Second Match

The oldest daughter, Mary Sangiolo, met her husband, Jim Molineaux,

through Josephine's sister-in-law and matchmaker,

Cay Sangiolo.

Cay knew Jim's stepmother Gert,

through the Franciscan Society,

made the introduction.

Mary and Jim married

and lived in the third-floor apartment owned by Tom and Josephine

on Bowdoin Street.

Tom bought the property thinking his children might need a place to live

when they married.

Mama Caterina

Mama Caterina developed dementia in her eighties.

In the fall of 1949, Josephine took her away from the farm

to live with them in Dorchester.

She was suffering from gallbladder disease,

wreaking havoc in her home,

spilling things

and driving everyone crazy.

It was time for her to leave Sunny View Farm.

A Blind Date

"My father wants to know when I'm going to ask you to marry me." Lou Sangiolo

Lou and Marie met on a blind date. Marie's friend Teresa was going out, and her date was friends with Louis Sangiolo. They called him to ask if he wanted to join them. They were going to the Magna Movie Theatre to see a show. They stopped in to get him and Marie noticed "he hadn't shaved in days; he was nothing to look at."

Tom and Josephine were in Duxbury, and Lou had to work late that night. Lou told them to go ahead without him, and he would meet them later. When he arrived at 10 pm he had shaved and cleaned up nicely, *not bad, Marie thought to herself*. They finished watching the movie and then walked to get an ice cream at Brigham's.

After that, Lou called her twice for another date, but she already had plans. Lou was lost, beside himself, did not know what to do without another date with Marie. Teresa called Marie on his behalf to say that Lou wanted to go out again, but she was always busy.

Marie told her, "Tell him to call me again." After three weeks Lou said, "My father wants to know when I am going to ask you to marry me." Marie responded,

"Are you asking me to marry you?"

Lou was so quiet, he never talked! He was smitten. Louis had found his match.

They were engaged after six months, Lou asked if she could cook pasta.
Marie replied, "Pasta? What kind of pasta do you like? Spaghetti, ravioli, tortellini, lasagna?"

Josephine never made lasagna. Marie had to teach her how to make it. Lou was in love with Marie and her lasagna.

Marie and Lou Sangiolo 1949

Marie (Longo) Sangiolo

"Marie puo' fare tutto," (Marie can do anything), said Marie's grandmother Corrao when meeting Louis for the first time.

Every day, Lou asked Catherine to play Lui Prima's song "Bella Bella Marie"

on the piano for him.

When the sun goes down, and the shadows fall,

I can hear a melody haunting me from over the sea,

I hear it start something in my heart,

Seems to say,' Come back again, come back to old Capri,'

Bella, Bella, Bella Marie, You're the fairest oh my Bella Marie,

Bella, bella, bella Marie, You are divine.

Marie and Lou married on April 16, 1950.

Marie worked in a factory sewing piece work for ten cents apiece.

Lou worked in the store until one day a customer helped him get a job

at the Boston Gas Company as a meter repair man.

He earned $48 per week.

Their first Christmas, Marie was so excited to spend it with the Sangiolo family.

Nonna Caterina De Lorenzo died suddenly on Christmas Eve, December 24, 1949.

Bowdoin Street, 1951

Marie Sangiolo and Mary Molineaux

sisters-in-law,

equal in beauty and strength.

Marie said, "I think I'm pregnant."

Mary said, "You can 't be pregnant,

I want to be pregnant first!"

Marie was due in May,

and Mary was due in June.

1952

Gaetano, Tom, Sangiolo outside his store

Tom sat in his chair outside the store,

watching his customers leave, one by one,

to shop at the A & P across the street.

      He loved to wrap every pear.

He loved his store, his customers, his work.

Emotional and financial stress was making him sick.

He was 59 and having heart issues.

His doctor put him on an all-rice diet to lose weight.

He and Josephine made plans to retire.

They were building a Cape house in Duxbury

on three acres given to them by her brother, John De Lorenzo.

That night, he was not well, but he would not go to the doctor.

He woke up with indigestion in the middle of the night,

sent Josephine away for an extra pillow and a glass of water.

When she returned, her lover was gone.

He had suffered a massive heart attack,

      at 59 years old in 1952.

At 53 years old Josephine became a widow.

Retirement: 3 Acres and a Cape, 1952

Josephine in front of her retirement home in Duxbury

Lou and Marie lived downstairs from Mary and Jim on Bowdoin Street.

Josephine called Lou that night to come and help her with the store in the morning.

Lou took a leave of absence from the gas company

To help his mother in the store

while she settled her husband's affairs.

On the weekends, Lou and her brother Anthony helped the builder finish the Cape.

Little Tom was only 14.

After a year, Josephine sold the store and the building on Washington Street

and moved to Duxbury.

Tom and Josephine were going to retire here, together,

At 53, she was a widow and a single mother.

Tommy went to Duxbury High School.

Uncle John helped her raise their youngest son,

a city boy in the country.

I Wanted to Know

by Maria Sangiolo

I wanted to know what happened the night my grandfather passed away,

had a cerebral hemorrhage and died, in an instant, gone.

I wanted to know my paternal grandfather, his beliefs,

his laugh, his sense of humor, his heart.

My parents always said, "You would have loved him Maria, and he would have loved you."

Encouraging words and familiar stories cannot fill the void of a missing grandfather.

I wanted to know how his son, his baby boy,

felt without a father at fourteen.

But I was wrong to ask.

Who wants to remember such a night?

Who wants to open that book, look

at the pain of that sorry night?

Fourteen with no father

no brother or sister at home.

Alone.

The youngest boy, a teenager, alone

with his widowed mother.

I was wrong to ask.

Chapter Five: Second Generation - In Their Own Words

La buona salute e la vera ricchezza

"If you're healthy, you're wealthy." Louis Sangiolo

Louis, Mary, Joseph, Josephine (Ma), Catherine, and Thomas Sangiolo

"I have three perfect sons and two daughters." Josephine (Giuseppina) Sangiolo

Twenty-five dollars

by Catherine Sangiolo, Sitting in a restaurant in Taormina, Sicily 2013

Oh, it started in New York. We were both hired to work for Eastern Airlines. This was the start of commercial aviation, really, and it was 1951. I was there in New York.

I left Dorchester US of A, and my mother was like, "Padre, santo, spirito, Mama Mia, you going where? To New York?"

"Yah, I got a job Ma."

"Eighteen. Eighteen. Ok. So, what's the matter with you? We don't give you enough to eat. You've got a roof over your head. You going to where? New York City?"

It was a sin city you know.

"Who did you know in New York?" asked Uncle Tom.

"I didn't know anyone!" said Aunt Catherine. "But I had a job. I had a job, and I went to work in New York, and I was eighteen and very stupid, very, very stupid. I did not know anything. I think my father gave me twenty-five dollars. I did not know anybody there."

Here I am in the city of New York working for Eastern Airlines. It was about the third day, and I did not have any money. I was living in the YMCA, and I had a roommate named Syd, God bless her, and the two of us were pioneers really! I don't know anything other than being stupid, we were pioneers. Every day we would go to the employee lounge in the office, and there was an honor system where you could help yourself to a cup of coffee and a donut. We ran out of change and at that time I think we were puttin' buttons in. Anything that made a clinking noise in the honor box system! Three times a day, it really was sad because we were hungry.

One day I sat beside this woman who was painting her nails in the employee lounge. And I loved painted nails, but I can't really wear them now 'cause the polish eats my skin. Anyway, I'm sitting there, and I said to her,

"What colah is that?"

She looked at me, and said, "Pink. You are not from New York are you. How old are you? Does your mother and father know that you are living here in New York?"

I said, "Yes," and I was getting really annoyed.

She said, "Do you have a place to live?"

I replied, "Well yes, we are living at the Y, but we are looking for an apartment."

And I'm thinking to myself, *who is this chick and who died and left her in charge of my life, so I left.*

The next day I came back to the lounge, and she sought me out, she really did, and said, "Look, if you are interested, my mother has a couple of rooms that she doesn't use anymore, you can room and rent them."

I said, "Well I'll ask my roommates."

I really didn't know if they would be interested. Anita's mother rented the rooms to us, we all accepted, and I went to live in Anita's mother's house. Mary had one room, and Syd and I lived in the other room. This was in Corona, NY, Queens, New York, the beginning part of Long Island. We took the train to work.

In the meantime, my mother and father were very worried about me, they really were, my mother, she was very upset. I was eighteen years old, and I just left, really! Anita and I became very close friends, we chirped and chirped and talked and talked. Her mother was Italian, and my parents were in Boston. I got the idea to bring Anita home to meet my parents at Christmas time and then they wouldn't worry so much, she would tell them that I was fine. I was well and living in New York.

I loved my job working for the airlines, it was really hip, and I knew my parents would have settled, so I brought Anita home. At the time, I was dating this guy, his name was Nick, and it was Christmas time and thought, you know, Nick might have a friend and we'd go out on a double date. He called all his friends and none of them were available. And I thought, *I could call Charlie Kurker.*

Anita said, "Well, what about your brother Joe?" I thought, my brother Joe, homely Joe? And Joe said, "Yeah, what about me?" He was home for the weekend from Akron, Ohio. And so began the love story of Anita and Joe Sangiolo.

Remembering Sundays
by Louis Sangiolo

Pa took over the kitchen on Sunday mornings, Ma used to tell everyone he soiled every pot and pan she had and naturally she was the one who had to clean up the mess my father made. Sunday morning was my father's time to shine in the kitchen. His specialty was making the sauce for the Sunday afternoon meal. Sunday's activities were consistent. Joe and I walked to church for an early mass at St. Peters in the Meeting House Hill section of Dorchester. The walk took us about a half hour. The church was about a half mile from our home. We went to Sunday school after church and then walked home.

Mom and Dad went to the 11:30 mass, and we usually ate dinner in the early afternoon. Our father had a store on Washington Street. We lived in an apartment above the store.

After dinner on Sundays, we almost always went to visit our grandparents and uncles and aunts in Duxbury. I vaguely remember the car my father had before the 1930 Ford Model A. The vehicle before the Model A Ford was a long station wagon, and it was open in the back and had a roof that extended over the back. I don't remember ever driving it, but I remember it parked in front of the store on Washington Street. The model A 'Woody' Station Wagon was quite a car. I don't think it had a heater when my father bought it. On the other hand, maybe the heater was an option because it had a separate unit that was mounted on the inside wall, opposite the front passenger seat.

In the wintertime, we in the back seats did not know that the heater existed. Coming home from Duxbury on Sunday nights, we used to huddle together with blankets. It was not a comfortable ride home on a cold, windy winter night. The windows of the Ford Station wagon were made of canvas and a brittle plastic called celluloid, the predecessor to plexiglass, and the windows had slotted holes around the edges that aligned with hardware mounted on the wooden frame on the upper part of the sides and body of the vehicle. There was plenty of fresh air entering the vehicle. In the summertime, the visits to the farm in Duxbury were very enjoyable. Joe and I always found something to do.

Little Tom Sangiolo

by Joseph Sangiolo

Tom was twelve when I left home to work in Akron, Ohio.

I used to tease him.

He liked to listen to Gene Autry on the radio and sit nearby on the floor,

listening intently, legs crossed, hands on his chin, just like Pa.

Autry was his big hero.

After the radio hour was over, Autry would say,

"You know folks, when me and the boys have a hard time at the ranch,

we reach for a stick of Wrigley's chewing gum.

There's nothing more that we like,

that makes the day go by,

than having a stick of Wrigley's Chewing Gum."

I would mimic Autry and smile and laugh, "You know folks…"

and Tom would laugh, too.

So bizzah, this big hero cowboy looking forward to a stick of chewing gum!

I gave Tom a carton of Wrigley's gum for his 80th birthday.

Catherine Sangiolo on Being Old:

"When you are old, you find a very straight chair with a straight strong back and you bend way over, and you put your head between your knees, and you kiss your ass goodbye."

My mother used to say, "If I ever lose my mind, take me out to the pasture and shoot me like an old horse."

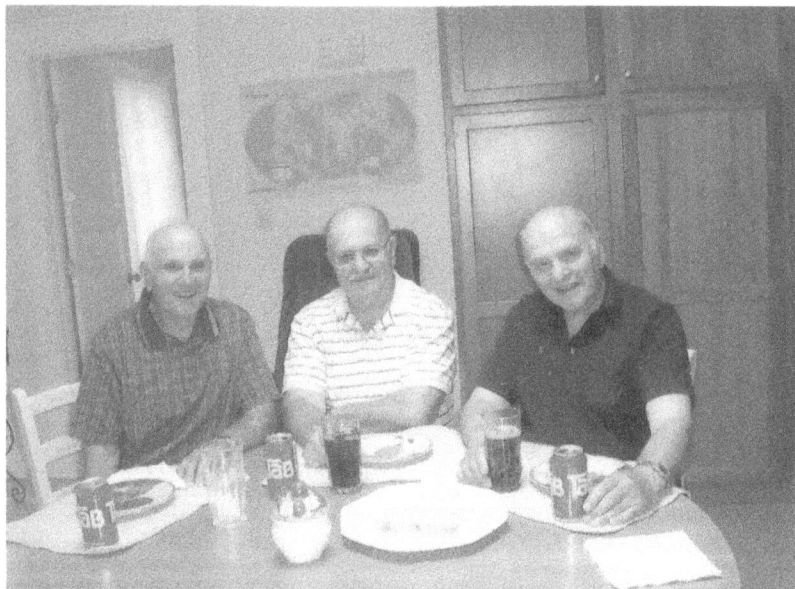

Louis, Tom, and Joe Sangiolo

The Eliot and Gould Radio Hour

by Uncle Tom Sangiolo

Little Tom Sangiolo and Louis Sangiolo on furlough from WWII

I remember when Joe would come home from school, and we would have lunch and listen to Bob and Ray on the radio. It was Bob Elliot and Ray Gould, and they used to have these bizzah songs they would sing, and one of them was, "Pull down the shades for I see you, pull down the shades for I see you, when your back goes passing by, I see you!"

When Louis Sangiolo Told the Story of the Big Fight

There were several turkey farms on Route 53 in Duxbury. Back then they called it Turkey Row. Anna and John married first and were living with the grandmother. Then Joe married Kay; he at the time was working with John. They lived in the farmhouse with my grandmother Caterina, Anna and John, Joseph, and Kay, two married couples.

Tears flood his voice box as he begins to try and speak. He pauses.

Mom says, "Here we go again."

"Ok, now I'm ready to tell my story. I'm going to guess I was just six or seven years old in my grandmother's house. (Crying) Big meeting, BIG MEETING between Anna, John, Joe and Kay, and my grandmother, and my Uncle Tony was up from Florida. He just happened to be there. Anyway, big brawl, big family argument. I was under the kitchen table hiding, so I ran outside away from the noise. His aging body now convulsing at the memory of it all, tears filling his throat, he could barely speak.

"I was there, they did not know it, but I was there, and I heard it all. It was terrible."

"I couldn't stand it; I ran out crying. Uncle Tony followed me, and he told me, 'Don't worry, everything is going to be all right.' And that is when the break off went, my grandmother broke up the land."

The Apparition
by Louis Sangiolo

Now I will tell you of an event that happened when I was just a little guy, and I've kept it to myself all these years (tears forming in his throat). I was probably between two and three years old. The living room had another entrance from the room beside it, and this room had another door that opened into the great hall. I ran from the great hall through this door and the door that led to the living room, and I stopped after I entered the living room. My grandmother, Maria Cafarella Sangiolo, my father's mother, was sitting in one of the living room chairs, her eyes closed, praying with her rosary beads in her hands. I looked up and saw an apparition of the Blessed Virgin Mary. I ran out of the room very frightened. I've never forgotten that, and as I said never mentioned it to anyone.

My paternal grandmother came to America sometime after my grandfather, Luigi Sangiolo, died. My grandmother spent time at the homes of her three children, Aunt Gianna and Uncle Frank Cafarella, Aunt Cay and Uncle Tony Restuccia, and with us. She did not speak very much English, so I do not remember that I talked with her at all. My sister Mary once told me that she taught us to speak Italian. After grandmother died in 1936, my parents very seldom spoke Italian in our home. They were very conscious of speaking English well because of the direct interface they had with customers in the store. They also were concerned that we learned the English language well. I regret that I did not insist that we learn to speak and understand Italian.

Rules
by Louis Sangiolo

We always had our meals together in the kitchen. That was one of the family rules. We always had the whole family at mealtimes. No exceptions! And there was another mealtime rule: 'NON SI MANGIA, NON SI PARLA.' No talking while you are eating.

Pa's (Gaetano's) Daily Trips to the Market

Papa Longo was thrilled to learn his daughter Marie was dating Gaetano Sangiolo' s son. Papa Long once said, "Everyone knew Gaetano in the market, he was a beloved businessman." Papa Longo was a fruit peddler there for many years in addition to working in the kitchen at Durgin-Park and other odd jobs.

Louis Sangiolo, March 2013

My father went to the market, the market in Boston, every day, whether he needed anything or not. He had to go to the market and see all his cronies and talk and whatever. Probably pick up a couple of things. And on the way home, he would come down Dorchester Avenue. Dorchester Avenue is a big street that comes right down into the market. He'd come home down Dorchester Avenue, and my aunt Cay and uncle Tony had a store there. What he would do was go in the store, get 'em to start fighting and then he'd leave. He'd get them into a big argument, and then he'd leave laughing. "I wish you knew him, Maria," said Mom, "Your uncle Tom is a lot like him, Tommy is just like him, sits at the table just like him, with his hands folded like this, just like his father."

Joe Sangiolo, August 28, 2013

I didn't tell the story of my father. On his trips to the market, he would stop at his sister Cay's store in Dorchester; it was right on the route. He'd stop in there, we would go in, and Aunt Cay would be by the cash register and my uncle Tony would be on the other side of the store. Dad would go in and say something to light a spark, and the next thing you know my aunt Cay would start yelling, going off on a tirade, swearing at her husband, "You dirty son of a bitch, bastard, God damn…" and my father would be there just chuckling. He'd get them all going, and then we would walk out. Laughing after he stirred up trouble.

(NOTE: Cay was a nickname for Catherine. There were so many Catherines in the family.)

Little Luigi
by Louis Sangiolo

I wandered away from my father during one of the many trips I took with him to the market in Boston when I was three or four years old. My father must have really been upset looking for me. I eventually was taken to the police station. I waited behind a wooden railing that separated a desk area from the rest of the room. I got all excited when I saw my father enter the room. The people in the station told my father that when they asked what my name was, my only response was "Luigi." You can bet that from that day forward my father never let me out of his sight during our trips to the market.

He left for the market at seven o'clock and got back just before noon. After my uncle Louis died, an elderly man named Nicolas (Natalie) Brandi came to live with us, and he helped my father in the store. He tended the store when my father went to the market on weekday mornings and Sunday. I really enjoyed going to the market with Pa. He usually bought fruits from a wholesaler named F. Cincotta & Sons. The Cincottas were a large family who also came from the island of Salina.

Louis, Joseph, and Mary Sangiolo

Soapbox Derby

by Joe Sangiolo

Mary and Louis

When we were growing up, they had that race, I forget what they called it, that race they have in Akron, Ohio.

Mark Sangiolo asked, "The Soapbox Derby?"

"Yes, that's it, in Akron, Ohio."

I worked in Akron and saw the hill where they used to race the Derby. That was a big thing when I was growing up and in fact, they used to sell kits, you could build a soapbox from these kits and enter your car in the race.

"My brothers had them, they built 'em from scratch, there wasn't going to be any buying a kit with my dad" said Linda DeLorenzo, having grown up on Sunny View Farm with her father John and mother Anna.

Oh yeah, well, Lou built one, kind of a soapbox thing from scratch one time. I remember he made the frame, covered it with linoleum and painted it, and had the steering wheel with ropes for brakes. That was one of his projects. He rode it down the steep end of Claybourne Street.

Of course, two years older, Lou could do everything better than I could, of course.

He was my hero. Baseball, he played a lot of baseball. He even went to Fenway Park for a "try out day" when the Red Sox were looking for young prospects from the local neighborhoods. But the Spartans wouldn't sign a release, which is why the Sox did not win the World Series back then.

Uncle Joe De Lorenzo: Fish, Veggies, and the Boston Red Sox

by Ron De Lorenzo

My father went fishing with Uncle John all the time. Back in the sixties and seventies there were tons of flounder in Duxbury Bay. The two of them came home from fishing and there was a pile of fish, and my mother Kay would complain, "How am I supposed to put up all this food?" But she did, she cleaned the fish and froze it, and we had fish to eat for months.

After Peg and I married, we would visit my parents, and my father would hand us cranberry boxes full of tomatoes, zucchini, eggplant. There was no way we could eat all the food he gave us from his garden. We would bring some of the vegetables to Peg's parents in Green Harbor. My mother would not want us to waste the food. She would have to put it all up, canning the peaches, cherries, pears. They had two apple trees, strawberries, and rhubarb.

One time my father took my son Bill fishing, and I asked him what he had for lunch that day.

Young Bill said, "Nonno made bologna and jelly sandwiches." He said, "I ate it, I didn't want Nono to feel bad."

My father used to take me out of school for the Boston Red Sox Opening Day at Fenway Park. (Uncle Joe was an avid Red Sox fan.) He paid $50 for the bleacher seats in 1967 for the World Series, second game. He was determined to be there for the game. My mother did not want him to go to a night game because he had to be up early to work the next day. She took the car to the South Shore Plaza with a friend, so we would not be able to drive into the city.

He and I took the truck with the farm plates. You're not supposed to take a farm truck off the property. We passed Mom on the highway going into Boston. You could see the steam coming out of her ears.

Italian Joke
by Aunt Catherine Sangiolo

An Italian comes to New York to eat at a very elegant restaurant. He says to the waitress, 'There's no fork on the table.' He's very upset and tells the waitress, 'Excuz a me, there's a no fork a on the table. I wan na fork a on the table.' The waitress says, 'You cannot fork on the table.'

Not So Sunny at Sunny View
by Linda De Lorenzo

Pop always asked, "Linda, you want a job?"

Pop always had a job for us to do. Everybody had jobs.

My brother Joe DeLorenzo and cousin, Tom Sangiolo,

would haul 100-pound grain bags across the yard,

pour into the hopper to feed the turkeys.

My job in summer was to collect eggs.

I hated that job! I was just a kid,

I was little, but I still had to bend down to get into the pen.

The ladies would peck at my little fingers.

They did not want to give up their treasure.

Sometimes, I would rush in quickly,

> then run out and declare, "No eggs today!"

Pop was the first of the boys to say he was American, no more Gianni.

He did not do the Italian thing.

He left that Italian behind; he naturalized as soon as possible.

He always thought through what he was going to say.

Whenever he opened his mouth, you listened.

Nona Caterina wanted a very formal living room.

Me and Sass had to go up the back stairs to our rooms and not disturb her.

My mom, Anna DeLorenzo, had to account for everything she bought at the store.

There were piles of small notebooks and ledgers upstairs.

If she overspent, the grandparents took it from next month's pay.

Sunday afternoon in Duxbury, 1930: Gaetano (Tom) Sangiolo, Anthony, Joe, John, and Josephine DeLorenzo

Remembering my Sister Catherine

by Joe Sangiolo

"All I remember about Cathy, she is sitting right here, was she wanted to go out a lot and couldn't. My father would not let her. He was very easy with Mary. But for some reason and maybe she can explain."

His son Mark asked, "Did Mary go out a lot?"

"Not a lot, but she had a lot more freedom I think than Cathy. And all I can remember is Cathy saying, 'But why, why can't I go out?' And he never gave her a reason."

"Because I said so," Cathy replied. "That was the reason I got."

"Oh, I see," said Joe. "That's kind of a universal reason handed down," Mark said.

"Yeah," Uncle Joe laughed.

"That's why I left when I was eighteen," said Cathy. "Because I had to go, and I still to this day, I absolutely love to travel that is my thing to do, I really love to travel. And I was so held back and restrained, very stifled, Oh God, as far back as I remember."

Joe said, "But you must have been around the age of 13 or 14?"

"Yes, I used to cry, but why, why can't I go? It did not make any sense. You were all taking a trip to Ohio, you were going to Ohio."

Joe said, "Mary and I went one time, I forgot that, yeah."

"And I did not understand why I couldn't go. There was no reason why I couldn't go," said Cathy.

Catherine and Joseph Sangiolo

Twenty-five Missions (ASCAP 2001)

song by Maria Sangiolo

My father was a gunner in the second World War,

flew twenty-five missions in the belly of a B-24.

He came home with medals after the victory.

He came home with an injury nobody could see.

> My father enlisted when he was just eighteen,

> wanted to be a pilot, that was his dream.

> But the air corps had enough pilots, so he learned to use a gun.

> In '43, he left MIT, until the job was done.

I grew up asking questions about my father's war.

Ever demanding what that damn war was for.

A yellow check came every week, it said disability.

After school, I'd get the mail, wondering what does this mean?

> When I asked my dad about the medals he earned.

> Said he was no hero, but now I know what he endured.

> Said he just did his job, did what he was told to do.

> That's my dad, ever humble, faithful and true.

He said he was only doing his job,

nothing special like the ones who gave their life to God.

But my father flew twenty-five missions, the most that you could fly,

Twenty-five missions and my father came home alive, my father survived.

Battle Fatigue and MIT

by Louis Sangiolo
September 2000, A note from my father

Hi Maria, I thought you might be interested in this. The guy I am writing to is the newly elected Secretary of the MIT Class of 1950. They put together a yearbook and he is chasing the guys with nothing next to their names.

Dear Joe D,

In response to your letter dated 24 August, I offer the following: I am not a graduate. In the past, I have not participated in any of the Class of 1950 activities. I do consider myself an alum because I did successfully complete the first year at MIT as a member of the Class of 2-46, which was one of the accelerated programs initiated by the government in the early '40s. I hesitate to give you input for the yearbook. On the other hand, I do not like having my name with nothing beside it. I graduated from English High School in June 1943 and entered MIT in August in a wartime accelerated program mandated by the U.S. Government. My eighteenth birthday arrived during the last month of the first year, so I was a candidate to be drafted in the service. I opted to volunteer for induction into the Air Force (Army Air Corps) in their Air Cadet Program with intentions to be a pilot. I, along with thousands of other volunteers, were "washed out" at the convenience of the government and were sent to Gunnery School because there was a dire need for gunners. The air war was rampant in Europe in preparation for the invasion that happened on June 6, 1944 (D-Day). I was sent home on a seven-day furlough after completing Basic Training at Greensboro, NC, and was given orders to go to Tyndell AFB, Panama City, FL, to attend Gunnery School. After Gunnery School I was given another week's furlough, and then I reported to Westover AFB, MA, to be assigned to a crew and then go to Chatham Field, Savannah, GA, for overseas training. During my short stay at Westover, that event that Art Chase told you about happened. I'm not too proud of it, so I will not discuss it. It was a sign of my immaturity.

We became a crew in August of 1944. There were ten of us: four officers, pilot, co-pilot, navigator, and bombardier. The enlisted men were flight engineer and assistant, radio operator and assistant, and armorer and assistant. Three of the guys went to their respective technical schools, and us three assistants just had Gunnery Training. We completed our training in November and received our orders to join the 14th Air Force in Italy. We were allowed to go home on furlough before we left. We were assigned a brand-new B-24 to fly overseas. We were ordered to Mitchell Field, NY, to pick up the new plane. My mother and father came to New York to see me before I left. I even had the opportunity to go to the Stage Door Canteen in New York while we were there. It was a fabulous club for military personnel. There was a song written about it. It went something like, 'I met my love at the Stage Door Canteen, her name was Eileen...'. If sister Mary were around, I'm sure she would remember the words.

Our port of embarkation was Bangor, Maine. Some of us went to the Bangor/Brewer Thanksgiving Day football game. From there our route to Italy was as follows: Goose Bay, Newfoundland, Reykjavik, Iceland, North Wales, Marrakech, North Africa, Tunis and finally Gioia D'ecole, Italy. We left the B-24 at the base at Gioia and were driven by truck to our destination: 460th Bomb Group, Spinazzola, Italy, 55 wing, 15 Air Force. We had completed twenty-five missions when the war ended in Europe in May 1945 and were sent back to the states. We were waiting to be assigned to the war in the Pacific when the bomb was dropped on Hiroshima. I was discharged in mid-November 1945.

I was very anxious to get back to Tech (MIT) and continue my education. As it turned out, I was not mentally ready to go back to school. I skipped many classes and did not keep up with the required studies. At the end of the term, I was informed that I could not return for the next term. Several weeks later, I had a breakdown and was committed to the VA Hospital in Bedford, MA. I was there for about twelve months. After I was discharged, it took a while for me to get adjusted to the outside world. One day a friend of mine asked me if I would like to go on a double date with him. He was going with this young lady (Teresa McKenna), and she thought it would be nice if we all went out together. As it turned out, this friend became my wife about two years later. She was the best thing that ever happened to me. As I look back now and wonder what my life would have been like if I did complete my studies at Tech, there is no way I would have met the wonderful woman that I have for a wife. So, I do not have any regrets that I did not graduate from the Class of 1950. We were married in April of 1950. We celebrated our 50th anniversary this year, and our five children gave us a wonderful party.

After we were married, I regretted that I had not finished school, so I applied for admission at the Lowell Institute School, was accepted and completed both their mechanical and electrical engineering Courses. I also completed advanced courses in Differential Calculus and Technical Report Writing. Then I applied for admission to Boston University, was accepted, and completed the requirements for a Bachelor of Science in Engineering Management, going to school three nights a week for four years. I received my BS in 1965, and four out of our five children came to my graduation. Our fifth child was born in 1967.

In 1949, the year before our marriage, I went to work for Boston Gas in their Meter Repair Shop. I started as a floor boy, and during the nine years I was there, I worked my way up to their top job, Class A meter repairer. My brother Joe, who graduated from MIT in 1951, was working for Goodyear in Ohio, returned to Massachusetts to work for Raytheon. In 1958, Raytheon opened a plant in Dighton, MA, and I applied for a position as a production engineer. I had started at Lowell at the time, and my brother Joe "opened the door" at Raytheon for me. I stayed there for four years, and when it appeared that layoffs were forthcoming because of a work slowdown, I applied for work at GTE at their manufacturing plant in Needham, MA, and was accepted as a Manufacturing Engineer. I stayed with GTE for twenty-seven years. I transferred into management in 1974 and eventually moved into program management and retired in 1990. Well, Joe, I hope I haven't bored you. That's my story. I consider myself a very lucky guy. I have a wonderful wife and five great healthy children who are all married, and we have twelve grandchildren. Our oldest grandchild is twenty-two and getting married next May.

When Joe Sangiolo Told the Story of When he was Expelled from MIT

I want to talk about my education. In those days, parents didn't pay attention to their kids at all. We went off to school and came home, they didn't know anything about what was going on. I had an easy time in school, junior high, high school. I didn't get straight As but I was pretty much on the honor roll, without any effort. And after I graduated, my brother Lou applied and got into MIT. I thought, I guess I should go to MIT. I didn't have the drive to be an engineer like my brother. His son Mark asked, "Uncle Lou Sangiolo was accepted to MIT?'" Yeah, he went there for a year before he went into the Army. So, I thought well, I'll go there too. So, I went there and didn't expect it to be very hard. And not only that, but the thing that I also discovered was freedom. The professors didn't care if you attended class or not. I never even dreamed that this was how it was supposed to be, and as a result I'd hang around this club where all the commuters went. Hang there between classes. I learned to play bridge, ping pong, cut a few classes, and I found that things were not that easy, but I still didn't put in the effort. And so, I just scraped by. Mark asked, "That was your first semester?" Yeah, this was towards the end of the war 1945, I just turned seventeen years old. They had an accelerated course, so I went that summer, and I kept going, continued three straight terms in a row, just scraping by. And then I received a notice that they were throwing me out of school, I was being expelled. I couldn't believe it. Pa was very upset.

I discovered that there were three ways that you could flunk out. One was if you had very poor grades for one term. Another way was if you had two terms in a row that was not as bad as the first way, and then there was a third way. If you had been just scraping by for three terms, you were out too. I was kind of shocked, and I remember my father didn't react very much, but I'm sure he was disappointed. So, I figured what the hell; I'll just stay out for a term or two and then re-apply. Months later, I thought I'd re-apply, and much to my amazement they said no, I couldn't come back. Then I was really shattered; I was really in a quandary. I didn't know, I thought maybe I would go into the vegetable business. Mark said laughing, "We could have been vegetable magnates." Right, I'd show those Greeks next door, and we'd get meat and liquor and the whole thing. And I remember going into Boston, looking at different kinds of fixtures for the store and getting it all revved up. But my father wouldn't spend the money. His wife Anita laughing in the background said, "That sounds familiar."

Then I discovered that MIT had a night school called Lowell Institute and it was free. I applied there and started to study, started to do the homework. It was a miracle when you did the homework. I got good grades, and I re-applied to MIT. They said to come in for an interview; I sent them my grades and so forth. And much to my amazement, my father wanted to go with me. Aunt Mary had told Pa that he should write a letter to the dean on my behalf; Pa had never shown any interest at all. And he did, he came with me to see the dean. And I don't remember exactly what was said, but I think the dean was impressed that he was there. They gave me another shot, provisional; I had to do extremely well, I had to get good grades. It was summer again, and I took four courses for the term, did the homework, lost all contact with the Spartans, hah, living at home and commuting on the train, still working a little at the store, but not as much. I did all the homework, and I did well the last two years. "Did you lose any time? Took you a little bit longer?" asked Mark. Did I have to take an extra term? No, I got some credit for the stuff I did at Lowell Institute, and I ended up going two full terms, plus that summer. I don't think I did an extra term or anything. Because I had passed all my other subjects, just barely. And that was it and went on and did very well and got on the Dean's List.

There were a lot of family members who went to MIT. Three of De Lorenzo boys went there. Maybe Uncle Lou did it because Uncle Bart went there and graduated. Uncle Tony went there. I did it because Lou did it. Uncle Lou was more driven. He really wanted to be an engineer. "He must have been bummed when he got drafted," said Mark. No, it was different then, everyone was involved in the war everyone. Everyone went. He didn't get drafted, he joined before he got drafted. "It was amazing that the De Lorenzo boys all had an education," said his wife, Anita. "That generation, which was unusual, four boys raised on a farm, all the uncles."

Remembering Dorchester

by Tom Sangiolo, Westford, MA

Tom Sangiolo and his son Thomas

Growing up in Dorchester I never sensed that we were immigrant children. The only time my parents spoke in Italian was when they did not want us kids to know what they were saying. I never heard my parents swear in English, but my mother swore in Italian. I confronted her on this matter in my later teens when she burned her finger and cried out an expletive in Italian and I said, "Ma, that was a terrible swear." She did not know that I had learned the word. Her comment was, "That's okay Tommy, God doesn't understand Italian."

We only had one phone in the house and one in the store and they were both on the same party line. Customers would phone in orders. My father would fill them, and my brothers would deliver them. One customer complained to my father that she couldn't get through on a call, and he knew the phone in the store was not being used. It did not take him long to figure out that my sister Cathy was guilty. The phone had a rotary dial. Dad put a lock on it to prevent it from dialing to keep Cathy off the phone. This did not stop her as somehow; she figured out by pressing on the receiver she could dial a number. The system was simple: one press was a zero, two quick presses a one and three a two, etc. You always had to pause between numbers. I don't remember if my father ever found this out.

Dorchester

by Louis Sangiolo
An unfinished list of story ideas for his memoirs.

1) Making Mom's clothesline

2) The field behind the store

3) Girls calling for Joe in the backyard.

4) The Hut in the backyard that Joe and I built.

5) Fran Early and I grow flowers for a business venture.

6) The go-cart #7

7) Flooding the back yard

8) Making go-cart with carriage wheel, scooter, and roller skates.

9) Making things on the floor of my father's store when he was waiting on customers.

10) Making a work bench and organizing the room in the cellar as a shop.

11) Writing the scores of the Spartan's basketball games on the wall of the back room in the stone cellar.

Feast Day of Saint Bartolomeo

by T. Bart DeLorenzo, Hollywood, California

When I visited Salina for the first time in 1989, I was traveling with a friend, and we did not make any arrangements ahead of time. We arrived in Lipari and there were crowds of people. We inquired at the Visitor Center near the ferry landing about lodging. There were three young college students staffing the counter.

A young woman said, "I'm sorry signore, there are no rooms available. The island is booked solid. Have you tried Salina?" Bart said, "I am here to visit my ancestral home in Malfa, and we do not have a place to stay on Salina." The women asked for his name, "Come ti chiami?" He replied, "Bart DeLorenzo."

The girl nearly fainted when she heard his name and asked him to stay right there, and that she would be right back. He had arrived on the Feast Day of Saint Bartolomeo, the patron saint of the Aeolian Islands. She secured him and his friend a room, for free, and did not ask him any other questions.

Luigi Sangiolo and the Great Storm

by Alfred Restuccia
(Told to him by Maria Cafarella, mother of Luigi, Cay, Gaetano, and Giannina Sangiolo)

Nonna Sangiolo always wore black skirts and black robes mourning her husband, Luigi. After he died in 1919, she came to America and took turns staying with her three children. But she stayed at her son Gaetano's home most often.

She once told Alfred Restuccia, "There was a great storm off the island of Salina, and the people of Capo Faro were so scared they entered a cave at the side of the mountain, all huddled together, waiting for the storm to pass." Luigi Sangiolo, my grandfather was a lay person but faithful and highly respected in the village because he owned so much land on the mountain, goats, and sheep. He raised the children on goat's milk. He and his wife would shear the Merino sheep's' long wood, card, and spin it into yarn. They were not simple peasants. When you owned a ship and land, you were called a Don, a man of power and great wealth, 'molto famoso.'

She said, "Luigi left the cave and went out into the elements, winds blowing and the seas so high they almost touched the cave. He prayed and spoke to the Gods asking them to protect his people, asking the storm to pass and save them. And moments later, the storm passed. The villagers were eternally grateful to him for saving their lives and their homes." They buried him in the old chapel in Capo Faro.

For at least three hundred years, the Sangiolo family has lived on the island. They fled the Inquisition in Spain when people, accused as heathens, fled for their lives. Tony Cincotta, Lou Sangiolo' s godfather, said the same, that "the Sangiuolo/Vasquez branch originated from Spain." Our cousin Antonello Sangiolo said the family came from the Campagna region of Italy.

Sister Mary, 1998
by Louis Sangiolo

Sister Mary was a special person, very loving and caring. She loved people, enjoyed a good laugh, and loved to sing and dance. She was always ready to help people. Mary had so many talents, including sewing, dressmaking, and she was an excellent cook. But she had another characteristic that most family members do not know. My big sister became aggressive at an early age, and my brother Joe and I were the first victims if we did not follow her instructions. She did not hesitate to give us a punch in the ribs or on one of our arms. Mary continued these acts of leadership, until Joe and I grew big enough to rebel and punch back. When she realized that we could punch hard or harder, she stopped punching us and proceeded to develop into a young lady.

Mary completed high school at Jeremiah E. Burke High School and improved her secretarial skills by completing an intensive course at the Boston Clerical School. She worked for at least two companies before her marriage in 1948. She raised five children. and shortly after her fifth baby was born, she became a single mother. Mary raised her five children with meager funds and never asked for help. I can remember her working at a local variety store to make a few dollars to help pay the bills. She eventually got an excellent job at the State House. My sister did a remarkable job raising her five children, and she did it all alone.

After her retirement from the State House, she became the family leader again. She was the one who made all the telephone calls to all the siblings to check that all was well with the family. When she recently changed her telephone service to one that permitted her to call anywhere in Eastern Massachusetts she was in her glory. Mary and I talked on the phone often. I shall miss her very much.

Goldilocks and the Three Bears

by Yusuf De Lorenzo

I remember them building your Noni's Cape house.

The room I remember most was the kitchen.

Josephine, Big Sis, had me stand there and watch her cooking.

She knew I would get into some kind of mischief.

Dad was helping Uncle Lou with rolls of tarpaper, finishing the roof.

She turned to me, lifting the spoon of meatballs and sauce,

serving a bowl of spaghetti and said,

      "Look, it's like Goldilocks and the three bears."

Strands of pasta and three different-sized meatballs,

one for each of us.

Sundays were great.

For years, we used to alternate Sunday dinners,

between our house, my father Tony's, Uncle John's, and your Noni's.

It was more than wonderful.

The Italian's Grape Juice

by Peg DeLorenzo (wife of Ron DeLorenzo)

My mother warned me that Italians like to drink wine. She said, "It will be their own homemade wine, so don't drink it or it will kill you."   Ron brought me home to dinner to meet his folks, Uncle Joe, and Aunt Kay, for the first time. Kay put a large, two-liter Ginger Ale bottle on the table. I did not drink it for fear of my life. The next time we went to dinner, a jug of red liquid sat on the table. Kay asked her, "Don't you like to drink cranberry juice?"

After that, the wine came out in the Ginger Ale bottle, and Ron's father poured himself a glass after dinner.

Recipe for Duxbury Red

by Uncle Tom Sangiolo

Duxbury Red was a blend of grapes, consisting of a ratio of 4 to 2 to 1.

Grenache, Muscato and Concord, respectively.

We bought the grapes at Don Gandolfo's market in Chelsea, MA.

Uncle John had his own Concord grapes.

I believe the final product was about 12% alcohol.

The Concord grapes, believe it or not, are very low in sugar

Which lowers the alcohol percentage.

But I liked the taste of that ratio.

It is similar to Valpolicella.

Uncle John on How to Keep a Happy Marriage

(during his speech at Linda and Leonard's wedding)

1. Never go to bed mad at each other.
2. You must always communicate with one another.
3. The third thing - he could never remember number three – sex?

The Mayflower and Mr. Nixon, 1957
by Linda De Lorenzo

The Mayflower II landed at Plymouth Rock

a gift from Plymouth, England

an emblem of friendship

between American and British soldiers

who served during WWII.

I sat by the water in front of the cottage,

with my best friend, front row seats,

waiting to see the great sails round the corner

of Plymouth Harbor.

Dad is home with Mom,

Preparing.

Nixon is coming to town, his man.

Unbeknownst to him,

the Vice President pays the farm a visit

on the way home to Boston Airport

via Route 53, the only road

from Boston to the Cape in 1957.

After the parade

in which he admonishes the crowds

with his dirty grin and fake waves,

his team of security guards drive him to Sunny View Farm.

Security men take over the place.

Mom and Pop are inside the

newly opened street front

to sell the turkeys to the public.

Dad is smitten with pride.

He gives out all the turkeys in stock,

one for the Vice President and all his men.

Nixon gives Pop a photo for the wall saying, "Thanks for the tasty turkeys."

Nixon stayed on that wall until 1968 when he was elected President.

Pop sent the photo to the White House,

asked him to sign it again, since he had a new job now.

Nixon obliged and sent it back to Pop.

Not sure where that faded photo went.

Pop and my brother Joe fought all the time about the Vietnam War.

Gaetano Sangiolo, too, could not understand.

Why did his brother-in-law like the crooked politician?

Uncle John

by my sister Louise Sangiolo Devin

Uncle John De Lorenzo, Aunt Edna De Lorenzo, Noni, and Aunt Anna De Lorenzo, 1987

Uncle John was my hero, notable because he spoke little except of course when he had something important to share or teach, often doing so in an impish way, like Noni. The other uncles were not as well known to me, only seeing them in passing during family affairs. John, however, as you know, had the turkey farm, and his home was a hub for our family.

Fishing trips with him were a tradition. When I was old enough to drive and lived on my own, I would reach out for a "date" with him on his little boat. It included a bucket of bait, poles, a barrel of veggies, and a jug of his homemade wine, all crucial ingredients for a perfect outing. When the fish weren't taking the bait, a swig of wine would work wonders, and our luck returned. On the way back to shore, the veggies were to feed the seagulls from our hands. "Take and give as you go," he would say. This was more than a fishing trip for me. In my twenties, he grounded me with a simple memory of what makes a given day and moment special.

In successive trips, I would include a current beau to assess, by his mannerism, what he thought of who I brought along. Brian passed when he made him laugh. Brian broke something

169

during the first job he was given on the fishing trip, and Uncle John asked, "Are you sure about this guy?" but it was endearing not critical. Once home, the fish had to be cleaned, and Aunt Anna needed help in the kitchen; but not much because she simultaneously turned-out fresh pasta and lobster sauce to round out the feast. My last conversation with him was at his belated 90th birthday party. He was sitting near the back stoop. I yelled "Uncle John, I often talk about you to friends." He replied, "Now why would you do that?" That humble little man is forever in my heart.

Fishing with Uncle Joe and Uncle John
by my brother, Thomas Sangiolo

Well, here goes. Dad had brought me down to Duxbury early one Saturday morning. I had gotten instructions from Mom, like I get from my wife Mary Jane in two words: sensitivity training. Well, we packed up the poles, bait, a gallon of Duxbury red wine, two six-packs of Narragansett, and went out to an area around Bug Light. The Bug Light, officially known as Duxbury Pier Light or fondly, The Bug, is located on the channel that leads to Plymouth, Kingston, and Duxbury Harbors. That's what Uncle John called it. Bug Light was the first cast iron, caisson-style lighthouse built in the United States. Its light stands thirty-five' above high tide.

There was plenty of sand and flora in the Bay. Uncle John was helping me with the baiting of the hook, a flounder rig. I must have been around nine years old and a chubby half pint to boot. He was putting the bait on the hook, and he told me to spit on the hook. It was a sure-fire way to catch a flounder. Uncle Joe had put the beer in the water to chill for later. I think it was down too, because after drinking the wine, they seemed to forget where they had put it. When they started up the motor, a shredded six-pack was tied to the rope. From what I remember, they were not too happy.

Oh, and the fishing boat that we used is still sitting in Carl's backyard.

Uncle John, Fishing 1967

by Maria Sangiolo

The skipper greeted you with a grand 'Welcome!'

to his fine vessel

a twelve-foot dinghy,

complete with a motor

and large bucket, half full of water

for the latrine.

He instructed the ladies,

to use the facilities

whenever needed,

the men would turn their backs.

It was an all-day outing,

Fishing with Dad and Uncle John.

Mom needed time to herself to go shopping or tend to baby Carl,

so here I was, on Duxbury Bay,

seasick again.

When I fished with Uncle John,

my latrine was the ocean.

"Just let it go over the side!" he would say,

as I heaved and prayed for us to return to the shore.

Uncle Joe and Aunt Kay, the Cranberry Partnership

When their son, Ron De Lorenzo, once asked his dad why he was bald as a young boy, his father replied, "A hurricane came and blew away the chicken coop and my hair went with it."

Catherine Sangiolo once asked, "Aunt Kay, you have been married to Uncle Joe for a long time. What do you think makes a successful marriage?" Aunt Kay took a long time to answer. These were her words: "Well, Catherine, I've noticed when I look at married couples, if there is one boss in the relationship, that one boss is married to a dope." Catherine knew what she meant and did not laugh either, referring to her own marriage to Mario.

Catherine continued, "My Uncle Joe was a dear, sweet man. When I was a kid, I would sleep over at their house with my cousin, Catherine De Lorenzo, the painter. We would be silly girls, laughing in bed, telling stories. After a while, we would hear this booming voice from downstairs, 'Ok Catherine, it's time to go to bed!' One morning he had been out late playing cards and worked in the bogs all day. Aunt Kay looked after him. She would go down to the cranberry bogs and say, 'Come on Joe, time to come home.' He worked so hard, when he got into bed he would say, 'Good 'ole bed.'"

Uncle Joe De Lorenzo said, "Kay and I were partners. She was a wife, mother, construction companion, frost watcher, and general partner in growing, and she worked in real estate. We raised our kids to be independent. My wife and I figured that the environment of the family will make or break a kid. You must keep them busy, not say, here is ten dollars, have a fun time. Spend time with your family."

Uncle Bart, the Gemologist

by Maria Sangiolo

Uncle Bart was a Pied Piper to the Sangiolo kids, the most gregarious and extroverted of all the brothers.

I reach for the narrow cardboard jewelry box,

behind a collection of notecards in the back of my bureau,

tied white rubber band holding the edges together,

torn from when my children played with these precious stones,

same box of gems my parents gave me in fifth grade, a gift from Uncle Bart.

In 1975, my parents, Louis and Marie,

celebrated their 25th anniversary,

went to Hawaii with a stopover in San Francisco,

made a detour to visit Uncle Bart.

Dad's hero was a chemical engineer.

Became a gemologist in retirement.

That Christmas, I received a rock tumbler.

As a kid, I collected rocks, stamps, coins, but rocks were my favorite.

Uncle Bart gave that box of cut and polished rocks to me,

rough-cut pieces of opal, polished amber, petrified wood, jade, onyx,

an oval cut, polished fossil piece, looks like a mini-chicken frozen in time,

crescent, moon-shaped rhodonite and a tiger eye cut for a bolo tie,

treasures from Uncle Bart.

Uncle Tony, The Artist

Tar Kiln School, grade 3

Tony was movie-star handsome.

He painted murals on the kitchen walls of the farmhouse,

a visual artist and trained architect.

Hand lettering below, no stencils!

The Woman Who Planted Seeds
by Edna DeLorenzo

Caterina (Matarazzo) De Lorenzo

On a tiny speck of an island in the Tyrrhenian Sea, off the coast of western Italy, lived my mother-in-law, Caterina Matarazzo, born into a family that raised Malvasia grapes for winemaking.

She learned in early childhood that one truly reaps what they sow. Planting and harvesting became a way of life for this very industrious female. The love of the soil and the challenges of successfully growing things were in her very nature from an early age and were to remain with her for her entire life. She instilled this passion in her sons and her grandchildren, who even now, one hundred years later, show a remarkable affinity for making seeds sprout and flourish.

The Aeolian Islands are volcanic, and to clear rocks out of the rich, productive soil was no easy task. My mother-in-law never expected any task to be easy. Indeed, it was un-worthy of

176

her attention if it were. Small in stature and delicate of feature, she had the heart of a Goliath and soon developed a back as strong as any man on the island. Not least among her many admirable traits was her joy in producing overflowing baskets of fine vegetables for her family and neighbors. Any surplus, she would take to the market in the small town of Malfa. The people began to wait patiently for Caterina to arrive with her remarkable produce.

On into adulthood, while she married, bore, and raised five sons and a daughter, this little lady continued to tend her garden and toil, not only in the vineyards, but on the mountainside as well. There she picked the capers for export and gathered wood to heat the oven where she baked huge loaves of hard-crusted bread to delight her family and, again, off to market where ready buyers were waiting. Ever mindful of her daily prayers with a treasured rosary tucked safely in a pocket, any moment spent in rest from her labors she devoted to grateful thanks to our merciful father who provided the bounty of the earth which she received.

The feast days of the Holy Saints were her only respite from her toils. Arising before dawn, waking her second son from his slumbers, she set off for the celebrations that made her heart sing. Briskly walking along a narrow, winding mountain road with a sleepy, young boy trudging behind, John was her constant companion. A woman must never walk alone; she was among the first to arrive. Hanging over her arm was, of course, a basket of her delectable food to share with the others of the faithful.

And so, her life continued, until the age of forty-five. At that time, through mutual decree of her mother, her sister the nun, and the parish priest, she left her beloved island to join her husband in the vast land across the sea, America. An immigrant in mid-life with a large family to care for, she faced the strange new land with the same determination she had shown the rock- strewn island of her birth.

Her flock would survive and flourish. Never wasting an iota of her time, money, or energy, she plunged into raising a family of achievers. Her goal became one with which she had little knowledge, formal education for her sons. Knowing an opportunity when it presented itself, Caterina bustled her boys off to school. Faithful attendance and high grades were demands eagerly met by her fledgling Americans. From a one-room schoolhouse in rural Duxbury, Massachusetts, she planted another seed. Her boys would be the first from the tiny island left behind to receive a college education. This undertaking she accomplished through

177

her efforts in growing her beloved vegetables and adding a barnyard full of noisy, dusty chickens. With the help of her sturdy, growing sons and her devoted husband, the farm was soon known as Sunny View Farm. Erecting a roadside stand, Caterina began selling her produce to a steady flow of satisfied customers. In marketing, as in her views on education, she was a woman ahead of her time. Knowing the buyers she found in her newly adopted country wanted only the best of produce, she sold them exactly that, the absolute best.

Diligently working from dawn to dusk she planted, harvested, and marketed, as she had learned to do at an early age. Happy to be out of doors in all kinds of weather and to feel the good earth under her hands, she went on to plant in her sons the seeds of faith in God, trust in people, and a love for life. These seeds also flourished. Indeed, they were her finest crop. Seeing her sons well-educated and going on to firmly established lives gave Caterina De Lorenzo immense pleasure. Through her love of the land, her endless devotion to her church, the ability to adjust her life from one continent to another, and successfully raise a large family, she attained something all of us strive to find, peace and fulfillment in old age. With a rosary in her hands, she departed this world at age eighty-four on December 24, 1950, a woman who had truly reaped all she had sown and left behind a legacy of growth which still flourishes.

Salamander
May 2021, Maria Sangiolo

Cousin Linda De Lorenzo

sold twenty-seven acres

of old Sunny View Farm

to the Duxbury Conservation Commission.

Said they "found a blue-spotted salamander, Amystoma laterale,

an endangered species, on the property."

Same soil that sent four boys to college.

fed a family for over a century.

On Salina, our ancestral home,

I saw an Aeolian wall lizard, Podarcis raffonei

while sunning myself out on the veranda.

It climbed out of a stone wall onto my blanket.

Emblem of a species on the brink of extinction,

less than a few thousand remain, another victim of habitat loss, tourism.

Found on island t-shirts, shrubby vegetation, and rural gardens,

gardens like my great-grandmother's in Malfa, Salina.

Cousin Concettina De Lorenzo said the young women on Salina,

"Place a salamander, strategically

between a young bride's breasts,

to bring her marriage good luck."

Could the blue-spotted salamander in Duxbury, Massachusetts,

that endangered species,

be a stowaway from my grandmother's pyramidal trunk?

Is it a descendant from the rocky shores of Salina?

Chapter Six: Belonging – We Are Not Alone

The idea for this book began in grief and in sentimental longings for my father. But the writing process led me to remember that belonging is a human need, one that starts in the womb and is met at birth by loving parents and family members. **The experience of belonging is missing in our children's lives where the internet has replaced human connection. I invite you to sign their names on your family tree, together, at the front of this book.** My hope is that these trees remind us that despite our busy lives, we still belong to one another, and are eternally love by our ancestors, connected in our great family tree.

Family stories told person to person, adult to child, pass down a history and pass down a loving connection that we never lose. Even after that person has left this earth, we always have that relationship, we just cannot create new memories with them. We belong to our ancestral loved ones. As my favorite person on the planet, Aunt Catherine, loses her memory, I hold the experience of her telling these stories to me with so much love in my heart.

I am certain my cousins have their own versions of these tales. Their young friendships provided me with someone to play with, to learn from, and yes, connect with in later life. Having grown up in a big family, there was isolation with siblings much older and younger than I am. My extended family and cousins, and there were five my age, filled a void at family gatherings. Some of my loneliness dissipated with play time at clam bakes, reunions, summer picnics and Christmas parties. These outings were all instrumental in making and keeping relationships with cousins who became much-needed friends. I became a different person by having summer vacations at their homes in the city, the country, and by the beach. They opened my eyes to other worlds beyond my suburban existence and taught me about music, musical theater, and the arts in general. Aunt Anita Sangiolo invited me to be her costume person backstage one summer in Plymouth, which sparked my interest in theater. Aunt Catherine played the piano while Cousin Terese and I sang Broadway tunes, dreaming of one day living together in New York City. Cousin Mary Ann Molineaux invited me for sleepovers in the city of Dorchester where we walked to Carson Beach. Cousin Irene told me about her travels to Asia and created our family tree on Ancestry.com, which is included in this book. Cousins Tom and John Sangiolo came to my gigs in the Boston area when I was a touring musician.

Noni, our grandmother, loved us all unconditionally, and my cousins had equal time with her when she visited them on weekend holidays. I often wonder what she would say about the world and how it has changed since she left it, and would she have lived her life any differently if given a choice? The song, "Audience of Souls," by Emily Smith of Scotland, speaks to that question.

Audience of souls I'll sit here before you.
And I'll sing to you a song
Sing to you a song.

From wisdom that you've gained
What advice would you give me?
And what would you change?

If you had your life again, would you live it the same?
Tell me what would you change?
If you had your life again
Would you live it the same?
Tell me what would remain? And what would you change?

Tony, Bart, Joe, and John De Lorenzo

My paternal grandmother and great uncles were special people, so much so that I had to record what I remembered of them in these pages. They were Aeolians. Noni would say, "We are not like those people!" meaning the Mafia. As a child, I had an awareness that these uncles were very dear to my father. Like him, they were so warm and kind. When we visited the farm in Duxbury, I never wanted to leave. There was an old smell to the house. The furniture was antique, and the fireplace in the front room was bigger than any I had ever seen with large stones around the mantel. I could feel the history in that room where they once sat together, crocheting to pass time in winter by the warm fire. I wanted to hear the stories that lived in the walls, and so I began to ask questions.

Anna DeLorenzo Giannetti and her husband Larry were my only connection to her father, Great- Uncle Tom DeLorenzo. He died long before I was born. Anna had the most beautiful smile and light in her being. She never had children of her own but was always delighted to see our family of five kids. Her father was the one to first visit the fully furnished farmhouse in Duxbury advertised in *The Boston Globe*. He took the train from Boston, on the Old Colony Line, to Duxbury to see the property and paid the farmer with the money his mother, our great- Grandmother Caterina, saved.

Dad took us to the family farm, Uncle John's Farm, to visit on Sunday afternoons in the summer, mostly to go fishing with Uncle John or swim at Duxbury Town Beach. We drove in our Chevy station wagon, wooden boards rattling as its tires rolled across Powder Point Bridge. When we arrived at the farm the scent of grapevines permeated the back doorway. Uncle John greeted me by bending down low to reach my height. Smiling, his eyes a twinkle, he would say, "You have a squeaky kiss!" His hearing aids whistled as he grinned. Dad built a shed in our backyard with shingles Uncle John gave him from one of the chicken coups from Sunny View Farm. The walls smelled musty like aged manure. My sister Louise and our neighbor, Donna DiCorpo, played school in that shed all summer with me, their student, lining the windowsills with old leather chapter books.

Uncle Joe, who lived down the street, grew cranberries and was the true farmer of the family. Educated at UMass Aggie, he sported arms the size of tree stumps with muscles so big he could have been a weightlifter. He and his wife Katherine built their home together. His smile was so genuine, he was so handsome, she was so kind, I just fell in love with them.

When Uncle Bart, the engineer with a pipe hanging from his lip, would visit from California he sat in the farm kitchen reading a book in the sunshine. His metal lamp from MIT alighted my father's desk (and mine in high school). Dad always looked up to Bart and attended MIT to follow in his uncle's footsteps to become an engineer.

Uncle Tony was movie-star handsome like my father. He and Dad were known to be ladies' men in their youth. I sensed that at a youthful age, call it women's intuition. But he was also an artist, a like-minded soul. His portrait of the photo to the left hung in the kitchen along with others throughout the farmhouse. He was self-taught.

I heard stories about family members who died at age 59: Uncle Tom De Lorenzo, the oldest boy, Catherine DeLorenzo, Tom's daughter, and my paternal grandfather, Gaetano Sangiolo. My parents' generation feared that number. Everyone thought if you made it to fifty-nine you would live a long life. With my fingers crossed, I turned sixty this past December.

Noni - Mary Josephine 'Giuseppina' De Lorenzo Sangiolo

Green Beans

June 2021, Maria Sangiolo

I wonder if my Noni had pain in her knees,

if that's why she sat when we cleaned green beans.

Together, we sat at the kitchen table,

her hands working to the beat of the clock, one bean a second.

We sat, knives in hands,

snapping off tips, snipping off stems.

She told of how when she was a little girl,

she helped her mom with the five boys

while great gran worked the farm.

She would say, "Every time I take a bath, I shrink-a-like-a-wool."

She was four feet and round in the middle.

Her breasts hung like large, pointing torpedoes.

The skin of her arms jiggled like Jello

as she raised her hand to gather another bean.

Mom picked them fresh that morning,

and we were getting ready for dinner.

Noni was home for a weekend visit. In those moments, I knew she was mine.

She sang, "I'm a lonely little Petunia in an onion patch and all day long I cry, cry, cry."

She made me laugh and smile, with a grandmotherly love in which I could do no wrong.

She said, "My how you've grown," squeezing my cheeks.

Noni loved cleaning beans. Noni loved me, and we cleaned them together.

We finished our job, filling the colander to the top.

She carried them to the sink, waddling as she walked.

I wonder, did she have pain in her knees?

Where I Find My Father
December 2022, Maria Sangiolo

Bing Crosby sings, "I'll be Home for Christmas, you can count on me."

I could always count on my father being there, until stage four liver cancer took him in 2013.

Now, I find him in Uncle Joe's smile and Uncle Tom's laugh,

and the way Uncle Tom says, Cahl, with the Dorchester accent and asks,

"How's the girls?"

I find him in the lyrics of Frank Sinatra, Johnny Cash, Nat King Cole,

and when Aunt Catherine plays piano

as we gather to sing "The Twelve Days of Christmas "at the De Lorenzo-Sangiolo Christmas party,

uncles competing for "Five Golden Rings!"

I find him in Aunt Catherine's smile. Her chocolate brown eyes shine like her big brother.

I find him in her faith, her prayers, her belief in spirit.

 "In dio padre, figlio, e spirito santo."

My father walks beside me, above me,

 in the night sky on winter nights,

when the deep darkness reveals bright stars,

 small universes, lighting the way as I talk to him.

My father's hands live in the pine end tables in my living room,

whose design he copied from a magazine photo my mother found and asked,

    "Lou, can you build these?"

In two days, he cut, assembled, whitewashed and completed the job.

My father could do anything, build anything.

I find my father in my mother, who is still alive at almost ninety-five, who speaks his name,

    who still grieves,

        like me.

In almost ten years, there are seldom tears, except when my children mention Papa,

and I realize how much they miss him too.

"Papa loves you" I say, "Papa loves you."

Epilogue: The Last Green Valley

I live in a corner, The Quiet Corner of Connecticut, in a small, rural town of about four thousand people where we own a country cafe. Family farming is returning to this verdant place of hills and valleys which has a rich history of agriculture. There are three active dairy farms in town, but our local food comes from two entrepreneurial young people who care about healthy soil and vegetables with nutrients, who left their modern lives in big cities for a quieter life steeped in community. They farm locally and own CSAs, like Brett Slovick, now running Fowl Play Farm on the De Lorenzo conservation land. Brett sells pasture-raised poultry, honey, and veggies at the South Shore Farmer's Market. He is an enthusiastic regenerative farmer, despite the hardships farming can bring, and is teaching others how to grow their own food in suburban backyards. Linda De Lorenzo is pleased to see the De Lorenzo land in West Duxbury farmed again. Check out his Facebook page: Fowl Play Farm and Miss Bee Haven.

This quiet corner of Connecticut is also part of the Last Green Valley because it is the last dark corridor between Washington, D.C., and Boston. When I married at age 31 and moved to this place I was living in Somerville, a Boston-area neighborhood that had nightly gang shootings. I was in shock for the first few years and had difficulty adjusting to the quiet and solitude, nor did I have friends here except for a few fellow folk musicians.

My husband said he was going to convert me into a "country bumpkin" and in fact, over time, he was successful. The city had its culture, arts, and entertainment and was close to my family in the Boston area. It was difficult to create community when I was always working or traveling for work. Moving to the Valley forced me to slow down and get to know people and become a part of something meaningful, my own marriage and family, as well as a rich, local collection of interesting people who live big lives in these woods.

Our restaurant patrons became our mentors, friends, and surrogate parents over the years. They helped us navigate our career decisions, our real estate decisions, and most importantly, our parenting. They lent us their ears when we needed someone to listen and gave us constructive feedback when it was most necessary. Paul Aicher, a philanthropist, Betty Hale, an icon and promoter of the arts, Norm, and Claire Greenman, of Rogers Corporation, and

Brian Denehy, a renowned actor all guided us in their own unique ways. There were other lesser knowns like Madeline who never had children and Beth and John who sat at the same table and ordered the same lunch every day, told us silly jokes and asked about my singing. Eleanor Racette, the wallpaper lady, gave me antique folk songbooks and a lovely trim for my baby's room. When it came time for college decisions, two men, Jock McClellan and Paul Graseck, steered us in the right direction for both our kids. Sally Rogers and Howie Bursen brought so much music and love to our music venue and a solid friendship.

We are rich in community in this Quiet Corner. We are rich in culture, open space, and local farms. We notice the birds and the bees, and the seasonal beauty surrounded by so much open land. We are blessed to live in this 'Quiet Corner' we call home.

The De Lorenzo and Sangiolo family have persevered over the years in this country, far away from the island of Salina. The Phylloxera aphid changed all our lives and brought us to this land of opportunity thanks to our elders, who paved the way at a different time in history. I am eternally grateful to them for their courage, hard work, passion, and vision of a future of opportunity.

Acknowledgements

This work is the product of years of listening, recording, writing and re-writing, created with the encouragement and support I received from family, friends and writers. I am indebted to my monthly writer's group - Mary Archambault, Donna Dufresne, Paul Grasek and Richard Telford for their camaraderie, sense of humor, support and editorial feedback. Special thanks to Marcello Saija and the Museo Eoliano della Emigrazione in Malfa, Salina and Carolyn Ravenscroft and Tony Kelso of the Duxbury Historical Society for historical details.

For many years, I have asked many questions of my aunts, uncles, and cousins. I'm certain they enjoyed telling their stories, but my persistence was often tiresome. Thank you all for being willing to dig deep, tell the truth, and share personal parts of your life.

Writers in Northeast Connecticut and editors in the Boston area lent me their ears, eyes, and ideas. I especially want to thank my dear friend Carolyn Shute, Christine Kalafus, Judah Leblang, Lisette Rimer, Brian Devin, Yusuf De Lorenzo, Liz Noel and my daughter's former English teacher Jamie Shaw. Your words of wisdom were greatly appreciated as were your editorial comments. Extra special thanks to Erica Wheeler for her one day Roadmap Workshop.

Nancy McMerriman worked tirelessly on the family trees and cover design. My extended family are eternally grateful to you for this important work! Thank you for your kindness and friendship. Talia R. Jessurun painted the original watercolors. We had to print them in black and white due to a limited budget. Thank you, sweetie!

This book would never have been completed without the support and help of my life partner and husband, Barry Jessurun. He stood by me patiently as I researched and wrote for almost eight years and even traveled with me to Salina to do more research. (That was the fun part!) He helped me navigate Microsoft word, created the back cover layout and prepared the text for publication. I love you with all my being, always.

Aeolian Islands

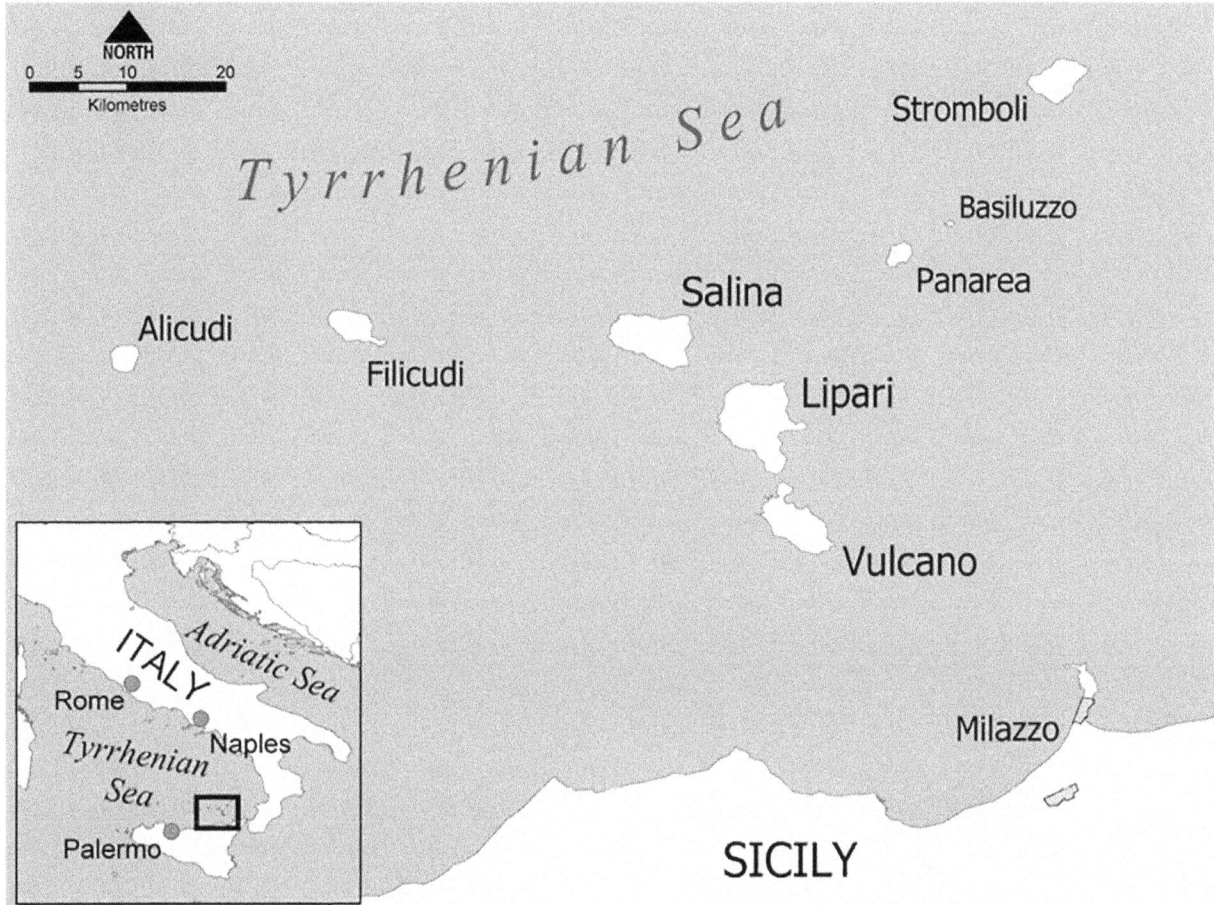

Stromboli

T y r r h e n i a n   S e a

Basiluzzo

Panarea

Salina

Alicudi

Filicudi

Lipari

Vulcano

NORTH

0   5   10   20

Kilometres

ITALY

Adriatic Sea

Rome

Naples

Tyrrhenian Sea

Palermo

Milazzo

SICILY

www.ingramcontent.com/pod-product-compliance
Lightning Source LLC
Chambersburg PA
CBHW041603260326
41914CB00011B/1367